WISDOM OF THE EAST

THE HEART OF INDIA

SKETCHES IN THE HISTORY OF HINDU RELIGION AND MORLALS

WISDOM OF THE EAST

THE HEART OF INDIA

SKETCHES IN THE HISTORY OF HINDU RELIGION AND MORLALS

BY

L. D. BARNETT, M.A. LITT. D.

PROFESSOR OF SANSKRIT AT UNIVERSITY COLLEGE, LONDON

GYAN

Published by

GYAN

Gyan Publishing House
5, Ansari Road
Daryaganj, New Delhi-110002
Phone: 011-47034999, 9811692060
E-mail: books@gyanbooks.com

Distribution Network
gyanbooks.com
India, USA, Canada, UK, Australia, France

ISBN : 978-81-212-2188-7 (HB)
First Published, 1908

2nd Impression 2021

Printed at: Gyan Press, Delhi.

Wisdom of the East, The Heart of India
Author: L. D. Barnett

WISDOM OF THE EAST

THE HEART OF INDIA

SKETCHES IN THE HISTORY OF HINDU RELIGION AND MORALS

BY

L. D. BARNETT, M.A., LITT.D.
PROFESSOR OF SANSKRIT AT UNIVERSITY COLLEGE, LONDON

LONDON
JOHN MURRAY, ALBEMARLE STREET, W.
1908

PREFACE

IN this little book I have brought together a few sketches of the things that are nearest to the heart of the millions of India. The heart is not the head, and therefore I have said but little of the great intellectual problems which have busied the Hindu brain for well-nigh two thousand years. But from the schools of the Pandits certain thoughts have gone forth which in a more or less vague form have become an integral part of the people's stock of ideas. Something therefore has been said of these, but not much. The main part of my task has been to shew what have been the worthiest answers given by the Hindus to the great questions of man's relation to God and to fellow-man. These answers have been many. Some are from learned schoolmen, like Sankara and Rāmānuja; others are from simple laymen, like Vēmana. But all of them are utterances of the vital faith of millions. We dare not ignore them.

If I have ventured to speak in condemnation of the unworthy legends which have gathered around the worship of Kṛishṇa, I have not done so without some warrant from the higher conscience of India. Only last year a distinguished native scholar, Mr. Chintaman V. Vaidya, wrote in his *Epic India* the following fearless words: "We entirely disbelieve the truth of these stories; no more mischievous though well-intentioned misrepresentations have ever sullied the fair name of a great man" (p. 422); and he adds further that "it is surely something exasperatingly inconsistent when those who recite Shrikrishna's *Bhagavadgita* . . . should themselves believe that Shrikrishna indulged in amours with the Gopis of Vrindavana which in others would at once be set down as deeply irreligious" (p. 446). To this I need add nothing.

CONTENTS

EDITORIAL NOTE

EDITORIAL NOTE

THE object of the Editors of this series is a very definite one. They desire above all things that, in their humble way, these books shall be the ambassadors of good-will and understanding between East and West—the old world of Thought and the new of Action. In this endeavour, and in their own sphere, they are but followers of the highest example in the land. They are confident that a deeper knowledge of the great ideals and lofty philosophy of Oriental thought may help to a revival of that true spirit of Charity which neither despises nor fears the nations of another creed and colour.

L. CRANMER-BYNG.
S. A. KAPADIA.

NORTHBROOK SOCIETY,
21, CROMWELL ROAD,
LONDON, S.W.

I. EAST AND WEST

TWO great Aryan races passed almost at the same time through the same course of thought. While the Greek mind was growing from the youthful realism of the Homeric Epos to the transcendental idealism of the older Eleatic school, the Hindus were rising from the level of the Ṛig-veda to that of the Upanishads. The old gods remained; but they no longer seemed to thoughtful men to embody the highest powers ruling over life. The great verities were now revealed to them in the laws of their own thought.

But in India the change was far deeper than in Greece. "You Hellenes are always children," said the greatest of their thinkers, "no Hellene is an old man." Here and there might be found a Greek who, like Plato and Parmenides, dared to turn his eyes from the semblances of experience; and at all times might be heard in Greece voices of despairing lamentation over the vanity of earthly things. But whether he rejoiced or wept over it, the true Hellene was of this world. In its experiences, glad or sad, lay all the reality that he could ever know. Nowhere do the two voices of the Greek spirit find finer utterance than in Pindar:

> A dream of a shadow
> Is man. But whenso honour
> Cometh given of Zeus,
> There dwelleth on men a bright light
> And pleasant life.*

But the Hindu surrendered the world. In the search for his own soul he denied one by one every principle of finite experience, from highest to lowest, and fearlessly drove reason to its last extreme of loneliest abstraction. From the schools he carried his doctrine forth into the world, and it grew almost into a national religion, with the creed "All is One—universal Thought without object—and that is my Self."

II. THE GODS OF THE ṚIG-VEDA

THE Ṛig-veda reveals to us a world very like that which meets us in the Homeric Epos. The Aryan tribes who have invaded the north-western corner of India are slowly spreading out towards the lower basin of the Ganges on the south-east

* *Pythia*, viii.

and the sea on the south—a slowly moving wave of fighting men loosely knit into warring clans and principalities ruled more or less effectually by chieftains and kings. Their livelihood is won normally by farming and cattle-rearing, regularly supplemented by pillage and raiding ; and law and order depend upon the energy of the local chieftain or the ability of the individual to take care of himself. As religious guides they have clans specially trained in ghostly lore ; foremost among them are certain families remarkable for traditional skill in framing hymns to be sung at the various rites, and from these has been compiled the Ṛig-veda. These priests live on the bounty of the rich, and do not dissimulate their by no means modest needs or desires ; their verses abound with covert hints or open demands for largesse.

Their gods are many and various. Commonly they are counted as 33 ; but one bold poet who gives the number at 3,339 does more justice to the theopoeic imagination of his race. In the forefront of their religion loom two mystic figures, the Sky-Father (*Dyaus*) and the Earth-Mother (*Pṛithivī*). Like their Greek counterparts Ouranos and Gaia, these shapes have come down from immemorial ages in mysterious indistinctness ; mythopoeic fancy, the surest token of man's love for his gods, has hardly touched these vast, incomprehensible, uninteresting realities.

It is not so with most of the other great gods. They are really "gods"—*devas*, "bright beings"—instinct with lively reality and vivid interest for their worshippers. Though in truth the chief of them seem to have been in origin embodiments of the powers of the sky, the process of personification has gone far and endowed them with human qualities that bring them into touch with man. Thus Mitra, Aryaman, Savitar, and Varuṇa all typify the sunlit heaven under one or another aspect; but they are no abstractions, they are the living genii of the sky, who sustain, stimulate, and guide the bustling world under a rule of law that is half-way towards morality. Varuṇa especially has become the divine counterpart of an earthly king, sitting in a heavenly palace, directing the ordinances of nature and maintaining by his judgments the rule of law in the world of men, which is traversed by his omnipresent spies. The fear of Varuṇa's vengeance for sin sometimes moves the poets to a higher strain:

Strong are creatures by the might of him
  Who hath established wide heaven and earth;
He hath cast asunder the vast broad sky
  And the stars; he spread out the earth.

I commune also with myself:
  "When shall I be at one with Varuṇa?
Will he accept my offering without wrath?
  When shall I in happiness behold him gracious?"

I inquire of this guilt, fain to see, O Varuṇa ;
  I come to ask of the wise men ;
The sages with one accord tell me :
  " This Varuṇa it is who is wroth with thee."

What is the exceeding sin, Varuṇa,
  That thou wouldst slay the friend who praiseth thee ?
Declare this to me, O potent one who may not be beguiled,
  That I may swiftly come guiltless to find thee.

Put away the backslidings of our fathers
  And those that are of our own works ;
O King, as the cattle-thief
  A calf from its tether, so do thou release Vasishṭha.*

The myth-weaving fancy, which hardly dared to touch these august figures, is however actively at work around the priests' darling, Agni the Fire-god. Agni is near and dear to every worshipper, for the sacred fires are lit in every house and burn in every sacrifice. Thus he is the deified priest, the guiding genius of ritual worship, the envoy of man to the gods ; and the priestly imagination puts forth all its ingenuity to convey these thoughts and to suggest the various modes of the Fire-god's manifestation in nature by laboured metaphors and cunning fantasy. It is characteristic of its general religious tone that the Ṛig-veda begins with a prayer to Agni as priest and bringer of wealth

Indra on the other hand is the type of the Indian warrior. He is in fact the Hindu Thor—

* *Ṛig-veda*, vii. 86.

a lusty, hard-drinking, strife-loving, mighty man of valour, the strong champion of the fighting Aryan tribes. When they address themselves to him—and only then—the Vedic poets rise sometimes to an almost epic vigour of narrative style. Like Thor, he seems to be in essence a genius of the thunder-cloud; and the story on which the poets dwell most often is that of his victory over the dragon who pent up the waters of the rain.

I will declare the manly deeds of Indra,
  The first which the Thunderbolt-bearer did;
He smote the Dragon, he let loose the waters,
  He pierced the bosoms of the mountains.

He smote the Dragon dwelling in the mountain;
  Tvashṭar framed for him the heavenly thunderbolt;
Streaming forth, like lowing kine,
  The waters went down straightway to the sea.

Bull-spirited, he chose the Soma,*
  He drank the pressed juice in the Trikadrukas †;
The Bounteous took his missile bolt,
  He smote this firstborn of the Dragons.

When thou smotest the firstborn of the Dragons, Indra,
  Then didst thou destroy the enchanters' devices;
Then, creating sun, heaven, dawn,
  Thou foundest at that time no foe.‡

* The fermented juice of a plant now unknown, which was much used to cause religious intoxication in Vedic rituals.

† A legendary rite, represented in the Vedic ceremony of the Abhiplava.

‡ *Ṛig-veda*, i. 32.

Legend has been equally busy with the figures of the two Aśvins, the bright gods of the dawn, whose gracious power has often rescued their worshippers from distress. The brief summaries of these stories which appear in the Ṛig-veda are fragments of a genuine old saga-cycle, a prehistoric "Acta Sanctorum," in which the Aśvins played the part of miraculous helpers in need to their devotees.*

The poetical feeling of the Hindus appears at its best in the hymns addressed to the deities who are merely personifications of the most brilliant phenomena of nature, as the Sun and the Dawn. Thus the former is described :

This sage god his beams bear aloft,
  The Sun, for all the world to see.
Yon stars like thieves flee at his light,
  Before the all-seeing Sun.
His beams, his rays have been beheld among the folk,
  Like glistening fires.

Swift, all-comely, light-maker art thou, O Sun,
  Thou enlightenest the whole bright world.
Before the families of the gods, before men, thou goest up,
  For vision of all light.†

And thus the poets go on, speaking often in commonplaces, but with real enthusiasm ; and

* The connection of the Aśvins with the Greek Dioskoroi, Kastor and Polydeukes, is possible, but very uncertain.

† *Ṛig-veda*, i. 50.

they sing most melodiously when they greet Ushas, the Dawn-goddess. In the hymns to the Dawn there is scope even for their imagination, and they display often a genuine warmth * of fancy and delight in detail-painting.

With fortune shine forth upon us, O Dawn, daughter of Heaven,
With mighty splendour, O lustrous one, with wealth, bounteous goddess.

Horse-bringing, kine-bringing, well finding all things, they ofttimes have sped to shine.
Send forth blessings to me, O Dawn; stir up the bounty of the generous.

. . . . .

Maiden-like, gracious, Dawn cometh shewing kindness,
Bestirring all beings; foot-faring things go forth; she maketh birds to fly up.

She who breaketh up the gathering and sendeth forth men in business, the dewy one, brooketh not a resting-place.
The birds at thy dawning, O mighty one, fly forth and stay not still.

She hath ridden from afar, from the rising-place of the Sun;
This blessed Dawn cometh forth with an hundred cars toward men.

The whole world boweth for sight of her; gracious, she maketh light.
May Dawn, Heaven's bounteous daughter, shine away feud and enmities!

* This warmth, it must be confessed, sometimes carries them rather far; the Dawn is occasionally described in terms suggesting that the poets saw in her a deified courtesan.

O Dawn, beam thou with bright beam, daughter of Heaven,
Bringing us abundant fortune, shining forth on holy rites.

For the breath, the life of every being is with thee, when thou shinest forth, O gracious one;
Lustrous, marvellous of bounty, do thou with thy mighty ear hearken to our call.

O Dawn, do thou win thee power that is marvellous among mankind;
Bring therewith the righteous to the sacrifices, the guides who sing of thee.

Bring thou all the gods to drink the Soma from the sky, O Dawn;
Bestow on us praiseworthy possession of kine and horses, O Dawn, gain with goodly manhood.*

III. THE UNKNOWN GOD

THE Vedic religion, as presented to us in the Ṛig-veda, is not noble. Its gods are either imperfectly moralised abstractions or figures of crude humanity; even in their reverence for Varuṇa, the embodiment of order in the world, the poets' sense of subjection to law was far stronger than their love for the ruler, and soon faded away altogether.† In Indian metaphor, the gods are

* *Ṛig-veda,* i. 48.

† Already in the *Brāhmaṇas* Varuṇa appears as merely the god of the ocean.

the milch-kine of the faithful, the priests their milkers. Wealth and worldly welfare are the chief objects of religion, and these the poets demand for themselves and their patrons with wearisome insistence. The hymn is a *suvṛikti* or "good charm," calculated to allure the gods and win their favours by its technical skill and ingenious flattery, rather than to voice the longing of the prayerful soul for communion with a higher power.

Sometimes the priestly flatterers went so far as to bestow the epithet "one and only" (*eka*) upon any god whom they might wish to propitiate. This, however, was not merely cajolery. Whole groups of deities had come to share in common attributes, and thereby had almost lost their individuality; and moreover the thought was rising that all beings—gods, men, and the world—were but diverse phases of a single First Being. "There is one Being," says a poet *; "sages call it by many names." An early attempt was made to set up the worship of the Sun-god as embodiment of this primal force; and two of the names given to the latter—*Hiraṇya-garbha* or "Germ (or Babe) of Gold" and *Prajā-pati* or "Lord of Creatures"—are distinctly solar in origin. Another and a bolder myth was spun by a poet who identified primitive matter with *Purusha*, "Man," that is to say, an ideal human sacrifice offered by

* *Ṛig-veda*, i. 164, 46.

the gods.* The outlines of this pantheism are thus sketched by one of the greatest of Vedic poets :

The golden Babe arose first,
  He was born the one lord of whatso is ;
He holdeth up this earth and heaven—
  What god shall we serve with our offering ?

Giving spirit, giving power, whose ordinance
  All worship, of whom are the gods,
Of whom the shadow is deathlessness, of whom is Death—
  What god shall we serve with our offering ?

Who by his majesty is the one king
  Of the moving world that breathes and closes its eyes,
Who ruleth over it, two-footed and four-footed—
  What god shall we serve with our offering ?

Of whom, through his majesty, are these snowy mountains,
  Of whom, men say, is the sea with Rasā,†
Of whom are these sky-quarters, of whom these arms—
  What god shall we serve with our offering ?

By whom the awful heaven and steadfast earth,
  By whom the sky was fixed, by whom the firmament,
Who measured out the light-garth in the mid-world—
  What God shall we serve with our offering ?

* *Ṛig-veda*, x. 90. The sacrifice generally is a source of power over nature, and the human sacrifice is the most effectual of all ; hence the cosmogonic forces, greatest of all powers, must arise from an ideal human sacrifice offered by the gods. Thus the poet reasoned.

† The mythical river of the sky.

Toward whom Heaven and Earth, established by His helping,
  Look, trembling in spirit,
Over which the sun uprising shineth—
  What god shall we serve with our offering?

When the mighty waters came,
  Bringing the universal germ, begetting Fire,
Then arose the one Spirit of the Gods—
  What god shall we serve with our offering?

Who in his majesty looked upon the Waters
  That were bringing Power, begetting Sacrifice,
Who is the one God over the gods—
  What god shall we serve with our offering?

May he not harm us, who is the begetter of Earth,
  True of law, who begot Heaven,
Yea, who begot the bright mighty waters—
  What god shall we serve with our offering?

Lord of Creatures, none other save thee
  Containeth all these born beings.
May we have that in desire whereof we offer to thee;
  May we be lords of wealth! *

Thus before the end of the Vedic Age the Hindus had arrived at a bold pantheism which derived all the manifold forms of existence from a single primary substance.

* *Rig-veda*, x. 121.

IV. BRAHMA THE WORLD-IDEA

To halt here was impossible; the passage to idealism was inevitable, and the first steps were taken already by a Vedic poet.

Not-Being was not, Being was not then,
  Air was not, nor sky beyond.
What was the covering—where, in whose ward?
  Was there water, deep, profound?

Death was not, nor deathlessness then,
  No token was there of night or day.
The One breathed windless, of its own power;
  Beyond this there was naught whatsoever.

Darkness there was, hidden in darkness, at first;
  This universe was a tokenless flood.
When the living was covered by the void,
  By the power of Heat * was born the One.

Desire in the beginning came upon it,
  Which was the first seed of Thought.
The root of Being in Not-Being was found
  By sages tracing it with understanding in their hearts.

Was their line stretched out across,
  Or was it below, or was it above? †
Sowers of seed there were, Powers there were,
  Potency beneath, Energy beyond.

* *Tapas* (the Latin *tepor*), properly warmth, hence inward brooding, the generative power of Will.

† Referring to a legendary organisation of the world by divine sages.

Who knows in sooth, who may declare here,
  Whence this creation was born, whence it was?
The gods were later in the creating thereof;
  So who knows whence it arose?

Whence this creation arose,
  Whether He made it or not,
He who watches over it in the highest heaven
  Knows indeed—or haply knows not.*

These words clearly lay down a first principle of metaphysical thought, that the whole of Being is in ultimate essence above the conditions of empiric reality, beyond the finite laws of space, time, and causality. But there still remained a great step to be taken—the union of the universal object with the subject, the identification of this First Being, *Brahma*, with the Self or essential thought of every thinking being; and this was done by the authors of the early *Upanishads*. Hindu thought thereby arrived at a true idealism.

V. BRĀHMAṆAS AND UPANISHADS

THE Hindus passed from the realism of the Veda to the idealism of the Upanishads by way of the Brāhmaṇas. It was a strange bridge; for the Brāhmaṇas are the handbooks of the early

* *Ṛig-veda*, x. 129.

Brahmanic priestcraft which had grown up on the basis of the simpler Vedic rituals, a priestcraft perhaps more crassly material in spirit and in practice than any other in the records of literature. An immensely intricate web of ritual—often of the most gruesome and butcherly kind—was spun around the whole of Indian life, with the avowed object of forcing from the powers of nature the gifts of worldly welfare which were theirs to bestow; and the ghostly power of the Brahman became supreme in the land.

In the classical age the ideal life of the Brahman was divided into four stages or *āśramas*. In his youth he was a religious student, living under vows of chastity in attendance upon a teacher. He then married and maintained a household, observing in it all the elaborate ceremonies of orthodox ritual. The next stage, as he grew advanced in life, was to hand over his household to his son, and to become an anchorete in the forest. And then, as death came nearer, he stripped himself even of his last possessions and became a *sannyāsi*, wandering about in utter destitution with his thought set upon his approaching end.

In a general way these stages of life correspond to the divisions of the Brāhmaṇas. To the householder's life naturally belong the elaborate rituals of the *Brāhmaṇas* proper. Their appendices, the Āraṇyakas or "Forest-books," are appropriate to the simpler life of recluses in the woods, as they are largely concerned with fantastic allegories in explanation of the rituals of the Brāhmaṇas. And as the anchorite gradually became the mendicant ascetic gazing fixedly upon the Infinite which he was approaching, so the last sections of the Āraṇyakas form the oldest Upanishads, which begin with fantastic musings upon ritual and by degrees pass into bold idealism, the mature *Vedānta* or " Vedas' End."

VI. PRINCIPLES OF THE UPANISHADS

IN this transition the Hindu mind was leaving far behind it the simple standpoint of Vedic ethics. It was gradually assimilating an idea which has ever since been fundamental in Indian thought—an idea expressed in the two words *Saṃsāra* and *Karma*, that is to say, the doctrine of metempsychosis (*saṃsāra*, "wandering" of soul from body to body) in accordance with " work " (*karma*, the activity of the soul at any time in its finite experience). Each of the countless souls which tenant the universe passes through an everlasting cycle of repeated births and deaths in bodies of every kind; each incarnation, and each moment of experience therein, is the direct fruit of former works, and itself results in future experience, for ever and ever. And life, however fair it may seem, is in reality a bondage of everlasting sorrow, that comes to an end only in the case of the few elect spirits who win intuitive knowledge of the transcendent Reality, Brahma, and in that knowledge gain salvation and union with Him.

The sum of Upanishadic teaching * is then that *Brahma*, the cosmic Force manifested as a universe to the thought, is in essence one with that same thought, with the *Ātman* or Self. "The Brahma, the power which presents itself to us materialised in all existing things, which creates, sustains, preserves, and receives back into itself again all worlds, this eternal infinite divine power is identical with the Ātman, with that which, after stripping off everything external, we discover in ourselves as our real most essential being, our individual self, the soul. This identity of the Brahma and the Ātman, of God and the soul, is the fundamental thought of the entire doctrine of the Upanishads." † And this supreme Reality is beyond all conditions of finite thought, and is describable only in negatives. Thought can reach it only in inspired intuition, and having reached it, wins for

* A detailed account of the teaching of the *Upanishads* and of Śankara's exposition is to be found in the little volume entitled *Brahma-knowledge*, in this series.

† Deussen, *Philosophy of the Upanishads* (English translation), p. 39.

the soul its salvation, everlasting union with the absolute Brahma.

VII. THE WORDS OF THE PREACHER *

WHEN a man has lost his substance, or his wife, son, or father has died, he may feel the sadness of it and yet by meditation be able to cast off his sorrow. And as to this they tell this ancient tale, how a friendly Brahman came to Senajit and talked with him. Seeing this king overcome by sorrow for his son, distraught with grief and downcast in spirit, the Brahman spoke these words :

"Why art thou so utterly discomfited, why lamentest thou, when thou thyself art worthy of lament, inasmuch as men will lament for thee likewise and then must themselves go lamented down the same path ? Thou thyself, O king, and I and all who do homage to thee, shall all go thither whence we have come."

Senajit said : "What vision, what mortification, O Brahman, what meditation, O thou who art rich in penance, what knowledge and what

* This chapter is from the Mahābhārata, xii. chap. 174, vv. 7–55. Its philosophic value is slight; but it vigorously expresses the Hindu *Weltschmerz*, the weariness of life which is one of the mainsprings of Indian thought. The notes that it strikes are echoed in the heart of every Hindu.

scripture-lore hast thou gained that thou art not discomfited ? "

The Brahman said : " Look how creatures of the highest, midway, and lowest degrees are everywhere here enmeshed in grief because of their works. Even this my soul here is not mine ; or rather, the whole earth is mine, and as it is mine, so it belongs likewise to others ; thus I think, and abide undisturbed. Having gained this vision, I rejoice not and grieve not. As in the great ocean one piece of wood meets another, and after meeting they again part from one another, such is the meeting of creatures. Thus it is with children and children's children, with friends and kinsmen ; it is not well to have love for them, for parting from them is inevitable. Come hither from the dark and again gone back into the dark, another knows not thee, and thou knowest not him ; who then art thou, and what is anything, that thou lamentest for it ? From the stress of desire arises grief, from the stress of grief arises pleasure, and from pleasure again arises grief, and again grief. The immediate issue of pleasure is grief, the immediate issue of grief is pleasure ; pleasure and grief among men roll round like a wheel. When thou hast passed from pleasure into grief, thou wilt thence pass once more into pleasure ; men cannot for ever have grief, nor for ever have pleasure. The body is the seat alike of grief and of pleasure. Life also arises together with this body; both wax together, and both together decay. Men are held by the manifold snares of the desires in the world of sense, and they fall away without winning to their end, like dykes of sand in water. Like sesame-grains for their oil, all things are ground out in the mill-wheel of creation by the oil-grinders, to wit, the taints arising from ignorance, which fasten upon them. The husband gathers to himself evil works on account of his wife; but he alone is therefore afflicted with taints, which cling to man alike in the world beyond and in this. All men are attached to children, wives, and kin; they sink down in the slimy sea of sorrows, like age-worn forest-elephants. On the loss of children, on the loss of substance or of friends and kinsmen, men suffer exceeding anguish, like the fire of a burning forest, my lord. This whole world depends upon Fate in pleasure and pain, in birth and unborn being. Whether a man have friends or not, whether he have foes or allies, whether he be wise or void of wisdom, he gets his happiness through Fate. Friends suffice not to make one happy, nor foes to make one unhappy; wisdom suffices not to make one wealthy, wealth suffices not to make happy. Prudence is not enough to attain wealth, foolishness hinders not success; the wise man, not the fool, understands this course of the world's way. Fortune follows whomsoever she meets, the understanding and bold, the silly and cowardly, the dull and the wise, the weakly and the strong. The cow belongs to the calf, to the herdsman, to the master, and to the thief; to him who drinks her milk the cow verily belongs. The most foolish in the world and the most prudent easily win success; but he who stands midway between them is afflicted." . .

"Pleasure, when it is of the spirit of sloth, ends in grief; grief, when it is of the spirit of energy, leads to pleasure; prosperity and happiness dwell with the man of energy, not with the slothful. But whether it be pleasure or pain, sweet or bitter, a man should bear with what befalls, as it befalls, unconquered of spirit. A thousand motives of sorrow and a hundred motives of fear fall daily upon the erring, but not upon the wise. Grief touches not him who is understanding, who has won illumination, seeks for knowledge of scripture, and is free from envy, self-controlled, and master of his senses. The wise man should hold fast to this illumination and keep watch over his thoughts; then he knows how the world arises and dissolves, and no grief can touch him. Whatsoever be the cause whence may arise a grief or an affliction or a sorrow or a labour of spirit, a man should put away that from which these may spring, even though it were a limb of his own body.* Whenever any work is done from a spirit

* Cf. Matthew, v. 29: "And if thy right eye causeth thee to stumble, pluck it out, and cast it from thee."

of selfishness, in the issue it becomes a source of grief. Whatever desires are cast out, their place is filled up by happiness ; but the man who runs after desires falls into destruction after his desires. All happiness that may come from fulfilment of wishes in the world, and all the exceeding bliss that there may be in heaven, do not together weigh the sixteenth part of the happiness that consists in the destruction of desire. On the head of each man, be he wise or foolish or valiant, comes every good and evil work that has been done by him in former incarnation, according to the manner of its doing. Thus truly all these sweets and bitternesses, sorrows and joys in souls roll round and round. Holding fast to this illumination, the good man sits in peace. He should guard himself from all desires ; he should cast desires behind him. Wrath is the name of him who stirs in the heart, who when strengthened is as death dwelling in the spirit ; abiding in the bodies of embodied beings, thus is he named by the wise. When a man has drawn inwards the desires from all sides, as the tortoise gathers in its limbs, he shall behold the light of the Self as his Self in himself. When one fears none and none fear him, when he desires no longer and hates no longer, he passes into Brahma. When he surrenders alike the true and the untrue, sorrow and joy, fear and courage, when he leaves behind him the sweet and the bitter, he will live in peace of soul. When he in wisdom does no kind of hurt to any creatures, either in work or in thought or in words, he passes into Brahma. Desire is a sickness that is hard for the foolish to abandon, which ages not with man's ageing, which only ends with life itself; blessed is he who frees himself from it!"

VIII. THE HEAVENLY WAY *

A CERTAIN Brahman who delighted in reading the Veda had a wise son, by name Medhāvi.† Now this son, who had skill for salvation, religion, and worldly affairs, spoke thus to his father, the lover of Veda-lore: "Father, what should a wise and understanding man do? For the life of mankind soon fades away. Tell me, father, how it is in the issue, in due order, that I may fulfil my duty."

The father said: "My son, after a man has studied the Vedas as a disciple under the vows, he should seek to beget sons to pay the debt to his fathers; and then, after he has kindled the fire and fulfilled the rites of sacrifice according to rule, he should go into the forest and strive to become a saint."

* This chapter is a translation from the Mahābhārata, xii. chap. 175, vv. 3–38.

† *Medhāvi* signifies "wise."

The son said: "Seeing that the world is so afflicted and held in bar around, and the Unfailing ones are fleeing by, why speakest thou as though thou wert wise?"

The father said: "How should the world be afflicted, and by what is it held in bar around, and who are the Unfailing ones here that are fleeing by? Of what wouldst thou make me afraid?"

The son said: "By death the world is afflicted, by age it is held in bar, and the nights are the Unfailing ones that are ever coming and going. When I know that death cannot halt, what can I expect from walking in a cover of lore? If life grows ever shorter as night after night passes by, then the man of understanding may likewise find his days barren. Who could feel joy where he is like a fish in shallow water? Before he sees his desires fulfilled, death falls upon man. Death will seize upon him, while he is gathering flowers and his thought is turned elsewhere, even as a she-wolf seizes upon a lamb, and hasten away with his prey. This very day do what is to thy best profit; let not this hour pass over thy head; for death carries away a man ere yet his tasks are fulfilled. Rather should one do to-day the work of the morrow, rather in the forenoon the work of the afternoon; for death waits not, whether one has brought to an end his labour or not. Yea, who knows whose hour of death will be to-day.

Let even the youth accustom himself to do his duty, for life is frail. Fulfilled duty brings honour on earth and bliss in the world beyond. Possessed by delusion, a man toils for wife and child ; but whether he have fulfilled his purpose or not, he must surrender the enjoyment thereof. When one is blessed with children and flocks, and his heart is clinging unto them, death carries him away, as a tiger a sleeping deer. While he is still gathering, and while his desires are still unfulfilled, death carries him away, as a tiger an ox. While one is busied in strivings and gratifications, thinking 'this is done, this must be done, and this other matter is half done,' death overcomes him. . . . Be he weak or strong, a valiant man or a coward, foolish or prudent, death carries him away ere he has reached the goal of all his wishes. As death and age, sickness and sorrow, arising from many causes, attach to the body, how canst thou remain composed ? Death and age pursue all that are born for their destruction ; to these two all creatures, unmoving and moving alike, are subject. The town-dweller's love of wife is a door of death, but the forest is a meeting-place of the gods, says holy writ. The town-dweller's love of wife is a fettering snare ; the good break it and escape, the bad break it not. He who does no hurt to creatures either in thought or in word or by his body, gets likewise no hurt from the living things which take away life and possessions.

Without the Truth no man can ever defeat the assailing host of Death; untruth must be renounced, for in truth is the seat of immortality. Therefore he who walks under the vows of truth, and devotes himself to union with truth, and has a true scripture and is constantly self-controlled, overcomes death by the truth. Alike the need to die no more and the need to die have their foundation in bodily life. The need to die arises from delusion; from truth arises the need to die no more.* I, who do hurt to none, who long for truth, who have cast away desire and wrath, and am indifferent and content in pleasure and pain, shall become free from death, like one of the immortals. Rejoicing in peace as my sacrifice, self-controlled, abiding in the worship of Brahma, a saint offering the sacrifice of word, thought, and deed, I shall pass away by the sun's northern road.† How should one such as I bring a bloody sacrifice of beasts? the wise man bring living offerings bearing temporal fruit, like a devil? He

* "Truth," the clear comprehension of the unity of all existence with the Absolute (*Brahma*) and with the Self (*Átman*) brings the certainty that the possessor of it will never be born again, but after his next death will be absorbed for ever in Brahma. Those who do not comprehend this unity, and thus are possessed by "untruth," must be reborn again and again, until they obtain the saving knowledge.

† That is to say, he expects to pass after death by the "Way of the Gods" through the sun to Brahma, and never return to bodily incarnation. See *Brahma-knowledge*, p. 53, and the *Bhagavad-gītā*, viii. 23f.

who has utterly suppressed words and thoughts * for ever, who practises mortification, self-denial, and truth, verily wins the universe. No eye is peer to knowledge, no mortification to truth ; no sorrow is equal to passion, no happiness to self-denial. Born in my Self by my self, established in myself, albeit without offspring, I shall live in my Self alone ; offspring cannot save me. No wealth is so precious for a Brahman as concord, indifference, truthfulness, goodness, firmness, harmlessness, uprightness, and gradual withdrawing from works in their order. What should avail thee wealth, or kindred, or wives, O Brahman, since thou must die ? Seek thou the Self, which is lodged in its covert. Whither have thy fore-fathers and thy father gone ? "

IX. RELIGION OF SANKARA AND RĀMĀNUJA

By insistence upon the strict identity of soul and Brahma, and hence upon the utter illusiveness of the world of appearance, these Upanishadic doctrines grew into the Later Vedānta, of which the chief exponent is Sankara, the

* A reference to the practice of Yogis, who aim at absolute abstraction of thought, or, as we may term it, thought without thinking.

Āchārya or Master, who appears to have lived about the ninth century. Śankara's title has been well earned. His influence, extraordinary from the first, has steadily grown, and now dominates most of the schools of Indian philosophy. And his system, strangely enough, has been a bulwark of positive religion. For it takes up two standpoints. One is that of absolute reality, where there exists nothing but the universal subject, in which the self and Brahma are one; the other is that of practical experience, in which the empiric Soul is confronted by a world and a God. On this foundation both the great Churches could establish themselves anew, the Vishṇuites identifying the Supreme Being with Vishṇu, the Śivaites with Śiva; and even mystics could appeal to Śankara's authority for their silly letter-jugglery and licentious worship of the female forces of Nature. The religious attitude of Śankara is summed up in a fine verse ascribed to him:

> Though difference be none, I am of Thee,
> Not Thou, O Lord, of Me;
> For of the Sea is verily the Wave,
> Not of the Wave the Sea.

But there was another and not less ancient school, which clung to the texts of the Upanishads that seemed to make a distinction between the one Absolute Brahma, the multitude of individual souls, and the world of matter; and hence arose the doctrine of "qualified unity," *Viśishtādvaita*, in opposition to Śankara's *Advaita* or "unity." The chief champion of "qualified unity" was Rāmānuja, who is said to have been born in 1127 A.D. The last great school was the bold dualism of Madhva or Ānandatīrtha (born 1199 A.D.), who declared the Supreme Soul, the individual souls, and matter to be really and eternally distinct.

We have seen how the religion of India, beginning as a primitive nature-worship, hardened early into an official cult of crude materialism, while at the same time it gave scope for the play of a semi-philosophic imagination which at length grew into the irregular but vigorous idealism of the early Upanishads. This again has for the most part flowed into two great channels, the severe monism of Śankara and the poetical religion-philosophy of Rāmānuja. But meanwhile the great heart of the people had created a God after its own image—Vishṇu, the Almighty Preserver, who in His boundless tenderness for His suffering and erring children deigns to assume human form on earth age after age, that they may be drawn near to Him. And the heart of India beat in the philosophers; to justify religion, theology was created. The Vedānta of Śankara makes a practical distinction between the deity revealed to the human consciousness and the absolute All-being, and thus renders possible a worship of love towards Vishṇu. But it was the school of Rāmānuja that first blended into a full harmony the voices of reason and of devotion, by worshipping a Supreme of infinitely blessed qualities both in His heaven and as revealed to the soul of man in incarnate experience.

"The Lord of Fortune," * writes Rāmānuja in the prelude to his commentary on the Bhagavad-gītā—"whose essence is absolute negation of all evil, accordance with blessedness, and infinitude of knowledge and bliss—who is an ocean of multitudes of boundless and blest qualities of nature, to wit, transcendent knowledge, strength, majesty, vigour, power, and brilliance—whose divine form is a mine of splendour, beauty, comeliness, youth, and other boundless qualities accordant with His will, uniform, inconceivable, godlike, marvellous, constant, flawless, and unsurpassed . . . whose feet are everlastingly praised by countless saints accordant with His will in their essence, being, and activities, delighting solely in doing all service to Him, and possessing multitudes of infinite attributes, such as eternal flawless and unsurpassed knowledge, power and empire—whose dwelling is in the supreme heaven called The

* Śrī or Lakshmī, the wife of Vishṇu, typifying the activity of the Supreme in the finite world.

Imperishable, which is indefinable by speech or thought, accordant with His nature, diverse, various, boundless, abundant in objects, means, and seats of delight, infinite in wondrousness, in splendour, and in extent, everlasting and flawless—whose sport is the origination, maintenance, and dissolution of the whole universe full of endless diverse curious objects of enjoyment and multitudes of enjoyers—who is the Supreme Brahma, Supreme Spirit, and Nārāyaṇa,—after having created the universe from Brahmā down to stocks and stones, withdrew into His own nature, and thus became impervious to the meditations and worship of the gods, from Brahmā downwards, and of mankind. But as He is a great ocean of boundless grace, kindness, love, and generosity, He assumed various similar forms without putting away His own essential godlike nature, and time after time incarnated himself in the several worlds, granting to His worshippers rewards according to their desires, namely religion, riches, earthly love, and salvation, and descending not only with the purpose of relieving the burden of earth, but also to be accessible to men even such as we are, so revealing himself in the world as to be visible to the sight of all, and doing such other marvellous deeds as to ravish the hearts and eyes of all beings high and low."

Thus there are three great ideas which are artistically welded together by this brilliant philosopher-mystic. There is first the belief in a Primal Being who is indeed infinite, but infinite in qualities of goodness; secondly, the doctrine that in His love for His creatures the Supreme becomes incarnate in divers blessed forms to save men from sin and sorrow, and lead them to union with Him; and thirdly, the teaching that the Supreme may be reached by any suppliant, whatever be his birth or rank, who worships Him in perfect self-forgetting love. This doctrine of love was no new revelation to the Hindu; a spiritual ancestor of Rāmānuja, the great Yāmuna Āchārya, has left us a poem, the "Gem of Hymns," in which he cries—

Oh, fie on me, foul shameless wanton brute
  Craving the rank of servantship to Thee,
Which lieth far, O God! beyond the chief
  Of saintliest Souls, Brahmā or Mahādeo!

The vessel of a thousand sins, and plunged
  Deep in the heart of Life's outrageous sea,
I seek in Thee the refuge of despair;
  In mercy only, Hari, make me Thine.

Forlornly stray I through the storm of Life;
  Soul-wilderment blots blind the heavens' face,
Griefs manifold pour unassuaging rain—
  Turn but Thine eye, Lord Achyuta, on me.

Hear first my prayer—'tis no glozing lie,
  But all most holy truth. Shouldst Thou refrain
Thy mercy from me, elsewhere wilt Thou find
  No vessel needier of redeeming grace.

But for Thee I am masterless; save me
  There's none to earn Thy mercy. Since our fate
Weaveth this bond between us, Master mine,
  Oh, guard it well, and cast me not away!

Whoever and whatever be the Self
  That weareth quality of this and that
In bodied form of Me, myself to-day
  I dedicate before Thy lotus-feet.

Lord Mādhava, whatever Mine may be,
  Whatever I, is all and wholly Thine.
What offering can I bring, whose wakened soul
  Seeth all Being bond to Thee for aye?

X. THE WORSHIP OF VISHṆU

GODWARD love in utter self-surrender is thus the keynote of Vishṇuite religion. A nameless poet cries—

Oh, give me a love firm-set on Thee,
  Janārdan, and blind to gain;
I will joyfully turn from heavenward hopes,
  And on earth in the body remain.

To realise the intensity of this appeal we must

remember the Hindu's horror of the life of the flesh.

The claim of utter helplessness is often heard. "If I were not a grievous sinner," says one writer, "if I were not overcome with terror, if I were not given over to the lusts of the flesh, then what need were there to throw myself on Thy mercy?" And another writes—

> Dull-witted and unknowing I, nor skilled
> To frame Thee cunning verses of delight;
> Only a vessel for Thy pity, Sire.
> But let Thine ear receive the bitter cry
> Of helpless agony, and swiftly come
> To lay Thy foot upon my wretched head.

Not less insistent is the cry of two other passionate pilgrims—

> Unbid to enter, darkling here I wait,
> And shrilly plain my woe without the Gate.
> Oh, turn Thine ear in pity, Master mine,
> To hear the wail of this my sham'd estate!

> Dear Lord, no peer in misery have I,
> No peer hast Thou in grace.
> This binds us twain; and can'st Thou then deny
> To turn to me Thy face?

A religion of the heart like this is indifferent to formal rites. "Whether a man have bathed or not, whether he be cleansed or not," says a worshipper, "if he remember the Lotus-eyed

One, he is within and without pure"; and another asks, "What avail offerings, holy places, penances, or sacrifices to him in whose heart is the shrine of Hari's presence?"

Nor is it only in the Vishṇuite church that this voice of passion is heard. Of the Sivaites we shall speak presently; here we may cite a few verses from a favourite Jain hymn, the *Bhūpāla-stotra*, addressed to one of the twenty-four Redeemers who, according to Jain doctrine, have appeared in successive ages on earth, teaching mankind to spare all life, even of the lowest creatures, and to hasten the salvation of their souls by mortification of the body.

To Thee, whose footstool buds with serried beams
From gems of all god-emperors' stooping crowns,
Disperser of the banded powers of sin,
Friend of the threefold world, great Victor, hail!

Simple am I, O Lord, who supplicate
One void of passion's stain, fulfilled of end.
To votaries is given not the skill
To limn aright the features of their lords.

Master in heaven, Thou art present still
In this clear spirit that reflects Thy grace.
When mirrors hold his beams, doth not the sun,
Though far away, shine here within the house?

The sins that cling from birth to bodied souls
Fade all, and are no more, through praise of Thee.
Before the fiery sunlight's serried rays
How long can dreary darkness hold its place?

Saviour, supreme of mercy, Thou dost still
The folly-fever of Thy votaries' souls;
Yet though I bear Thy will upon my head,
In me it is not soothed, I wot not why.

Fain for salvation, I am come to Thee,
The guide to cross the forest-wilds of Life;
Wilt Thou not heed when Passion's robber band
Would snatch from me Thy Treasure's trinity? *

The potter Karma,† wielding folly's rod,
Whirling me round the restless wheel of birth,
Sets me, poor vessel, 'midst a crowd of griefs;
O, save me thence, Lord, Guardian of the World!

XI. RĀMA AND KṚISHṆA

In the Vishṇuite church there are two great cycles of legend, the heroes of which are Rāma and Kṛishṇa, both incarnations of Vishṇu. Rāma is for the men, Kṛishṇa for the women, says the Hindu adage. The story of Rāma is told first in the great epic of Vālmīki, the *Rāmāyaṇa*, of which the earliest parts were composed at least four centuries B.C. Rāma-chandra, with his half-brothers Bharata, Lakshmaṇa, and Śatrughna, were sons of King Daśaratha of Ayodhyā.

* Namely intellectual knowledge, intuitive insight, and godly conduct.

† See above, p. 26.

By his prowess in bending the giant bow of Janaka, King of Videha, Rāma won as his bride Sītā, Janaka's daughter. Owing to the intrigues of his stepmother he was exiled by Daśaratha, and with Sītā and Lakshmaṇa lived in the woods. Then Sītā was carried away by the demon-king Rāvaṇa to his palace in Lankā (Ceylon); and Rāma with the armies of Hanumān, the king of the monkeys, marched southward, bridged the straits, overthrew Rāvaṇa, brought home Sītā, and was crowned king in Ayodhyā. And afterwards, hearing the vulgar speak slightingly of Sītā's constancy in Rāvaṇa's palace, he sent her away to the hermitage of the sage Vālmīki, where she bore his sons Kuśa and Lava; and at length they were reunited and raised to heaven.

The legendary figure of Kṛishṇa is far less simple and noble. It is in fact a complex of several local divinities. The Mahābhārata, the great epic poem, represents him in its earlier portions as a wise and powerful prince aiding the Pāṇḍavas in their struggle to recover their lost kingdom, and in its later parts as an incarnation of the Supreme Deity. In these aspects he is primarily connected with Dwarka and the valley of the Indus. Another group of legends connects him with Mathura. Here he is a pastoral god, as a child playing around the herdsmen's huts, stealing his foster-mother's curds and performing other like pranks, as a youth playing ravishing melodies on his flute while the herdswomen dance around in amorous ecstasy—an extraordinarily beautiful, lovable, and at the same time lewd and licentious character, such as is naturally created when the gross fancies of peasants are transferred to literature.

Such are the central ideas in the two great currents of Vishṇuite religion. The worship of Rāma as the Supreme become man is one that in general makes for righteousness. It teaches pure love of man and God, chastity, and manly effort. The worship of Kṛishṇa as a moral force is more doubtful. It arouses visions often of exquisite tenderness and beauty; but in proportion as it lays stress upon the amorous adventures of the pastoral god Kṛishṇa as described in the *Bhāgavata-purāṇa* and kindred literature, it tends towards a deep sensualism of the spirit, and often of the body also, which culminates in the doctrines of Vallabhāchārya, a teacher who was born in 1478, and whose clergy claim a first share in every pleasure of the laity, including even the *jus primæ noctis*. But it is not always so. There have been pure and lofty-minded worshippers of Kṛishṇa; and of the greatest of these, Tukā-rām, we shall presently speak.

XII. THE VISHṆUITE REFORMERS: TULSĪ DĀS

HITHERTO we have quoted only from Sanskrit writings, the cultured garden of Indian literature; we now turn to the open fields of the people's speech and thought.

Some time towards the end of the fourteenth or the beginning of the fifteenth century there was a man named Rāmānanda, who was of the following of Rāmānuja. But he found his church too narrow, too closely fettered in the trammels of caste-prejudice and scholastic learning; and he broke away from them. He travelled northward to the lands of the Ganges, and there preached the gospel of Rāma's boundless love for men of every race and order. He spoke to them in their simple dialect; and among his twelve apostles were a leather-worker, a barber, a Moslem weaver, and a woman. From him went forth a mighty current of religious feeling, a Reformation in the true sense, which is to this day alive and active. Many lesser streams have flowed into it at divers times from divers sources, streams of Moslem, Christian, and Jewish thought; and often it has strayed into devious paths and stagnant by-waters. But its main teaching is still that of Rāmānanda: "No man asks of race or creed; if one worships Hari, he is Hari's own."

Among the countless preachers and singers whom this revival raised up, there is one whose name is on the lips of millions—Tulsī Dās, who gave to Northern India its Bible. His great poem, the *Rāma-charita-mānasa*, or "Lake of Rāma's Deeds," is known and quoted in almost every village in the Gangetic plains, and represents the loftiest ideals to which his church has risen in the conception of Rāma's character. Tulsī Dās was born in 1532, literally "under an unlucky star," and was therefore abandoned by his superstitious parents, who were Brahmans of the Sarayū-pārīṇa tribe. A wandering friar found the baby, and adopted and educated him. He grew up and married; but death robbed him of his only son, and he took the vows of a Vishṇuite order. He began to write his great poem at Awadh in 1575; in 1623 he died at Benares.

His work is dedicated in all humility to the Blessed Lord whose deeds it recounts:

Though rapturous lays befit his praise, who cleansed a world accurst,
Yet Tulsī's rivulet of rhyme may slake a traveller's thirst.
How pure and blest on Śiva's breast show the vile stains of earth!
So my poor song flows bright and strong illumed by Rāma's worth.*

* This and the following quotations from Tulsī's poem are taken from Mr. Growse's translation.

The deity whom he worships is the Infinite Being incarnate as Rāma. "There is one God," so he tells us, "passionless, formless, uncreated, the universal Soul, the Supreme Spirit, the All-pervading, whose shadow is the world; who has become incarnate and done many things, only for the love that he bears to his faithful people; all-gracious and compassionate to the humble; who in his mercy ever refrains from anger against those whom he loves and knows to be his own; restorer of the past; protector of the poor; all-good, all-powerful, the lord Raghurāj. In this belief the wise sing the glory of Hari, and their song thus becomes holy and meritorious."

The Supreme, typified as Rāma, is absolute Knowledge and Love. "There is no difference," says Tulsī, "between the material and the immaterial; so declare saints and sages, the Veda and the Purāṇas. The formless, invisible and uncreated Immaterial, out of love for the faithful, becomes materialised. How can this be? In the same way as water is crystallised into ice. But how can He be subject to sensual delusion, whose very name is like the sun to disperse the darkness of error? In Rāma, who is the Supreme Being and the sun of the world, the night of delusion can have no part whatever; and in the Lord, who is Himself true light, there can be no dawn of understanding; neither joy nor sorrow, knowledge nor ignorance; neither personal piety nor the sins of vanity and pride; but Rāma is the omnipresent god, the blissful Lord of all, the ancient of days. . . . Fools do not perceive their own error, but senselessly attribute delusion to the god; like simple folk, who seeing a clouded sky say that the sun itself is dim, or who gaze at the moon through their fingers and fancy they see it doubled. Delusion affects Rāma in the same way as smoke, or a cloud, or dust affects the brightness of the heavens. The five objects of sense, the organs of sense, the gods of sense, as well as the soul, are all in their degree possessed of intelligence; but the great enlightener of them all is the eternal Rāma, the lord of Avadh. Whatever in the world is susceptible of enlightenment Rāma enlightens; every delusion is subject to Him; in Him centre all knowledge and virtue; and by His truth the dulness of material creation shines bright as the Ideal."

Tulsī is thus something of a metaphysician. He uses the terms of Vedantic philosophy to express the idea that although the Supreme, infinite in goodness and love, may seem in his incarnation to be subject to fleshly frailty, He is really not so; the cause of this semblance is Māyā, the cosmic illusion by which man's vision of the Ideal is clouded and dazzled by the phantoms of an essentially unreal world of finite experience. "Is there any," he asks, "whom success has not paralysed? who has effectually discarded vanity and pride; whom the fever of youth has not overcome; whose glory has not been ruined by self-conceit; whom envy has not besmirched; whom the blast of sorrow has not shaken; whom the serpent of care has not bitten, or whom delusion has not affected? Is there any so well seasoned of frame that he has not been attacked by desire as a plank by the weevil? The desire of family, of wealth and of renown, is a threefold temptation; whose soul has it not sullied? These all are Māyā's suite; who can describe in full her illimitable might? Since Śiva and Brahmā stand in awe of her, why speak of other creatures? Māyā's formidable army is spread over the whole world; Love and the other Passions are her generals, Fraud, Deceit and Heresy her champions. . . . This Māyā, that sets the whole world a-dancing and whose actions no one can understand, is herself set dancing with all her troupe like an actress on the stage, by the play of the Lord's eyebrows. For Rāma is the totality of existence, knowledge, and bliss. . . . the Lord that indwelleth in every heart; the Supreme Spirit, effortless, passionless, imperishable; in Him delusion finds no sphere; does darkness attack the sun? For the sake of his faithful people the very god, our lord Rāma, has become incarnate as a king, and for our supreme sanctification has lived, as it were, the life of any ordinary man. As an actor in the course of his performance assumes a variety of dresses and exhibits different characters, but himself remains the same, such is Rāma's divertissement, a bewilderment to the demons, but a delight to the faithful. Sensual libertines in their dulness of soul impute the delusion to the Lord, like as when a man whose eyesight is in fault says that the moon is of a yellow colour. . . .

Rāma alone is absolute Intelligence; every creature, animate or inanimate, is subject to Māyā. If all had the same perfect intelligence, tell me what would be the difference between God and His creatures? The creature in his pride is subjected to Māyā. Māyā with all its phenomena is subject to God. The creature is dependent on others, the Deity is self-dependent; the creature is manifold, Rāma is one. Though the distinctions made by Māyā are false, without Hari's help they cannot be dispersed, whatever you may do. The wisest of men, who hopes for salvation without prayer to Rāma, is like a beast without tail and horns. Though sixteen full moons were to rise and all the starry host and the forests on every mountain were set on fire, night would not yield except to the sun. In like manner, without prayer to Hari the troubles incident to existence cannot be dispersed. Ignorance has no power over a servant of Hari; knowledge emanating from the Lord pervades his whole being. Therefore there is no destruction for a believer."

XIII. NĀNAK AND THE SIKHS

Tulsī Dās founded no sect; the faith that he preached was too broad and catholic to be confined within sectarian bounds. But there was a mystic of the same order whose teaching had an unexpected result. This was Bābā Nānak.

Nānak was born in the year 1469 near Dera Nanak, in the Panjab. His rugged verses, which form the greater part of the Ādi Granth of the Sikh church, preach a doctrine of Godward love and quietism even more marked perhaps than that of Tulsī Dās, and certainly more strongly tinged with the amorous symbolism of the Kṛishṇaite churches. But the history of a religion depends as much upon the character of the worshipper as upon the nature of its creed; and the Panjabi is not as other Hindus. After some years of peaceful growth, the church which Nānak had founded rose in arms to avenge the death of Arjun Mall, the fifth pontiff after him, who had been slain by the Mughal governor of Lahore. They took to the northern highlands, and there formed a warlike little commonwealth, which gradually grew into the great Sikh empire of Ranjīt Singh. Their name *Sīkh* (the Sanskrit *śishya*) means simply "disciples," namely of Nānak, whose peaceful sect has thus grown into the most warlike community in India.

The spirit of Nānak's teaching is shown in the following verses selected from his Jap-jī, the prayer recited by pious Sikhs every morning.*

There is but one God whose name is true, the Creator, devoid of fear and enmity, immortal, unborn, self-existent; by the favour of the Guru.†

The True One was in the beginning; the True One was in the primal age.
The True One is now also, O Nānak, the True One also shall be.

By thinking I cannot obtain a conception of Him, even though I think hundreds of thousands of times.
Even though I be silent and keep my attention firmly fixed on Him, I cannot preserve silence.
Hungry [for God], my hunger ceaseth not though I obtain the load of the worlds.
If man should have thousands and hundreds of thousands of devices, even one would not assist him [in obtaining God].
How shall man become true [before God]? How shall the veil of falsehood be rent?
By walking, O Nānak, according to the will of the Commander as preordained.

* The version is that of Mr. Macauliffe, in the *Journal of the Royal Asiatic Society* for 1900.

† *Guru* means "teacher," viz. Nānak and his successors, as incarnations of the Deity. Nānak's "Guru" is God Himself,

He is not established, nor is He created.
The pure one existeth by Himself.
They who worshipped Him have obtained honour.
Nānak, sing [the praises of] Him, who is the Treasury of excellences.
Sing and hear and put His love in your hearts.
[Thus] shall your sorrows be removed, and you shall be absorbed in Him who is the abode of happiness.
Under the Guru's instruction God's word [is heard]; under the Guru's instruction its knowledge is acquired; under the Guru's instruction man [learns that God] is everywhere contained.
The Guru is Śiva; the Guru is Vishṇu and Brahmā; the Guru is Pārvatī, Lakshmī, and Sarasvatī.*
If I knew Him, should I not describe Him? He cannot be described by words.
My Guru hath explained one thing to me—
That there is [but] one Bestower on all living beings; may I not forget Him!

Pilgrimage, austerities, mercy, and almsgiving on general and special occasions
Whoever performeth, [may obtain] some little honour.
But he who heareth and obeyeth and loveth [God] in his heart,
Shall wash off his [impurity] in the place of pilgrimage within him.
All virtues are thine, O Lord; none are mine.
There is no devotion without virtue.
From the Self-existent [proceeded] Māyā,† whence issued a word which produced Brahmā and the rest—
"Thou art true, Thou art beautiful, there is ever pleasure in Thy heart!"

* Pārvatī is the wife of the God Śiva, Lakshmī of Vishṇu, Sarasvatī of Brahmā.

† See above, p. 52.

What the time, what the epoch, what the lunar day, and what the week-day,
What the season, and what the month, when the world was created,
The pandits did not discover; had they done so, they would have recorded it in the Purāṇas.*
Nor did the kazis † discover it; had they done so, they would have recorded it in the Kur'ān.
Neither the jogī ‡ nor any other [mortal] knows the lunar day, or the week-day, or the season, or the month.
When the Creator fashioned the world [only] He Himself knoweth.
How shall I address Thee, O God? how shall I praise Thee? how shall I describe Thee? and how shall I know Thee?
Saith Nānak, everybody speaketh of Thee, one wiser than the other.
Great is the Lord, great is His name; [it is only] what He doeth that cometh to pass.
Nānak, he who is spiritually proud shall not be honoured on his arrival in the next world.

Praisers praise God, but have not acquired a knowledge of Him,
As rivers and streams fall into the sea, but know not [its extent].
Kings and emperors who possess oceans and mountains of property and wealth
Are not equal to the worm which forgetteth not God in its heart.

* A class of Sanskrit religious works, largely made up of myths.

† The Moslem scribes who wrote the Kur'ān.

‡ *Jogī*, in Sanskrit *yogī*, a name for any Hindu saint and magician.

Make contentment thine earrings, modesty and self-respect thy wallet, meditation the ashes [to smear on thy body].*
Make thy body, which is only a morsel for death, thy beggar's coat, and faith thy rule of life and thy staff.
Make association with all thine Ai Panth,† and the conquest of thy heart the conquest of the world.
Hail! Hail to Him,
The primal, the pure, without beginning, the indestructible the same in every age!

One Māyā in union [with] God gave birth to three acceptable children.
One of them is the creator, the second the provider, the third performeth the function of destroyer.‡
As it pleaseth God, He directeth them by His orders.
He beholdeth them, but is not seen by them. This is very marvellous.
Hail! Hail to Him,
The primal, the pure, without beginning, the indestructible, the same in every age!

Make continence thy furnace, forbearance thy goldsmith,
Understanding thine anvil, divine knowledge thy tools,
The fear [of God] thy bellows, austerities thy fire,
Divine love thy crucible, and melt God's name therein.
In such a true mint the Word shall be coined.
This is the practice of those on whom God looketh with an eye of favour.
Nānak, the Kind One, by a glance maketh them happy.

* This verse refers to the dress of the typical *jogī* (*yogī* or beggar-saint). The ashes usually are of burnt cow-dung.

† *i.e.* make the world your Church.

‡ The three are the deities Brahmā, Vishṇu, and Śiva respectively.

The air is the Guru, water our father, and the great earth our mother;
Day and night are our two nurses, male and female, who set the whole world a-playing.
Merits and demerits shall be read out in the presence of the judge.
According to men's acts, some shall be near and others distant [from God].
Those who have pondered on the Name and departed after the completion of their toil,
Shall have their countenances made bright, O Nānak; how many shall be emancipated in company with them!

XIV. TUKA RĀM

When we turn to the churches which pay more exclusive worship to the incarnation of Vishṇu as Kṛishṇa, we are impressed by a curious feature in Hindu theology, which is far more prominent here than in the Rāma-cult—the disconnection between the morality of the worshippers and of their deities. A Hindu is surprised, even shocked, when we call upon him to apply to his gods the same moral standard as he applies to his own life. He willingly admits that some of the deeds ascribed to his gods would be most sinful if performed by men; but they are done by gods, whose nature transcends the conditions of human thought, and therefore they cannot be judged. We saw how Tulsī Dās applies this theory to the innocent human character borne by Rāma. The character of Kṛishṇa, however, is by no means innocent. As a child he steals and lies, as a youth he is a chartered libertine. From time to time, indeed, attempts are made to whitewash this morally as well as physically dark god.* But the fact remains that the chief religious works of this church dwell with most lustful fervour of sensual detail upon the amours of Kṛishṇa; for instance, nothing could exceed the carnal realism with which Jaya-deva's *Gītagovinda*, the most brilliant poem of this order in the Sanskrit language, paints the union of the god with his mistress Rādhā. To explain allegorically such writings is beyond the mark; whatever their esoteric meaning may be, the fact that they exist at all is the shame of Indian religion. Nevertheless, there have been men—and women too—in whom the idea of Godhead was so pure and potent as to be undefiled by the filth of myth; and such a one was Tukā-rām, the Marathi poet and saint.

Tukā-rām, son of Bolhojī, was neither a priest nor a scholar, but a poor country shopkeeper, and a Sūdra by caste; the figures of speech with which he clinches his verse are often homely and rustic. Yet he has the pride of one who knows himself to be chosen for the service of Heaven.

* The name *Kṛishṇa* means black or swarthy; and in art he is usually painted dark blue.

When the great Marathi emperor Śivājī invited him to his court, Tukā-rām refused. "Look upon my modest speech," he wrote, "as a grace of Him who dwelleth in the hearts of all men; for we that have submitted ourselves to Pāṇḍuranga * are not poor or pitiable; Pāṇḍuranga guards and supports us; what are others compared to Him? What can I ask of thee, that I should see thee? I have brought to naught all worldly longings. My fief is Desirelessness, for which I have surrendered the land of Desire: as the chaste wife longs only to see her lord, such am I to Viṭṭhala. All the world is to me Viṭṭhala, naught else; thee likewise I behold in Him."

Tukā-rām was born about the year 1600. Like Tulsī Dās and many another spiritual congener, he found Fortune a hard stepmother. His business did not prosper. He married two wives; one died early, and the other, a bitter-tongued shrew, made his home very unhappy. So his heart turned to find comfort in the Divine Love, and he became a votary of the god of Pandharpur. His own sorrows filled him with a deep tenderness for his fellow-creatures. Religion was to him love towards God and man. "He who calleth the stricken and heavily burdened his own is the man of God; truly the Lord must abide with

* *Pāṇḍuranga* and *Viṭṭhala* are the titles under which Vishṇu-Kṛishṇa is worshipped in Pandharpur.

him. He that taketh the unprotected to his heart and doeth to a servant the same kindness as to his own children, saith Tukā, is assuredly the image of God."

"It is not hard to win salvation," he says, "for it may readily be found in the bundle on our back. If we will to have the delights of Faith, our desire shall be fulfilled. Thou, O God, givest to each his fit and meet portion; and I, acknowledging it to be good, gladly receive it. Saith Tukā: thou mayst give me the world, as thou wilt; but give me a home for my love." And in the same strain he writes again: "If thou lookest on the wife of thy neighbour as on thy mother, what loss is there? If thou chidest not thy neighbours and covetest not their riches, prithee doth it hurt thee? If thou utterest Rāma's name when thou sittest down, what toil is it? Saith Tukā: no other labours are needed for the winning of God." Worship with a clean and lowly heart, keep a charitable spirit, do kindness according to your powers—this is the easy way to heaven.

Tukā knocked loudly at the Gates of Prayer. "Where wilt Thou hide Thyself, my God," he cries, "when I claim my portion? The Holy Ones bear witness to Thy promise; they know these tokens. I will be as a creditor sitting at Thy door, and will not let Thee come in." "Like a beggar, I have taken my stand at the door. O

God, send me an alms of some sweetmeat of Thy love; let not the beggar importune Thee and return again and again. Saith Tukā: the true gift is what is given in return for naught." "I take refuge with Thee, O God, with all my soul, in body, speech, and thought. Naught else hath entrance into my mind; my desire is ever set upon Thee. A heavy burden do I bear; who can lift it save Thee, my God? I am Thy slave, Thou art my Lord; I have followed Thee from afar. Saith Tukā: I have made a distraint for debt; let us meet for the payment of my reckoning."

But of the Divine Love, that suffers not a sparrow to fall to the ground, Tukā had never a doubt. "It is needless to lay a child in the mother's arms; she draweth it towards her by her own instinct. Wherefore should I take thought? He that hath the charge will bear the burden. Unasked the mother keepeth sweetmeats for the child; in eating them herself she hath no pleasure. When it is busied in play, she seeketh and bringeth it in; she sitteth pressing it tightly to her breast. When it is sick, she is restless as parched corn on the fire. Tukā saith: take no thought for thy body; the Mother will not suffer the child to be harmed."

And he looked forward with joyful assurance to the crowning grace. "I have borne toil," he wrote, "in order that my last day may be sweet;

and now I have won assured repose. The unrest of desire is stilled within me. I rejoice in the outlay that I have made; by it I have gained good fortune. Saith Tukā: I have wedded the bride Salvation; now shall there be a four days' revel."

XV. MĀYĀ.*

WHEN he had gotten from his father in due order the purifications of brahmanhood, Mārkaṇḍeya read the scriptures and practised mortification and reading according to the law. Calm of spirit, he observed great vows; his hair was coiled in tresses, his clothing of bark; he carried a pitcher, a staff, a scapular, and a girdle, an antelope's skin, a rosary, and *kuśa* grass † for the furtherance of his discipline, and at morn and evening worshipped Hari in Fire, Sun, Master, Brahmans, and his own soul. Evening and morning he brought to his master the food he had begged, and in silence ate his single meal

* The following story I have rendered, with a few slight omissions, from the Sanskrit *Bhāgavata-purāṇa*, bk. xii., ch. 8–9 (based upon the *Mahābhārata*, bk. iii., ch. 188 foll.). Its author, a Hindu Dante *mutatis mutandis*, vividly pictures the *Māyā* or phantasmagoria of finite life, across the lurid darkness of which falls a ray of light from the figure of the Saviour. Compare p. 52.

† The regular equipment of the Brahman hermit.

when given leave by the master; otherwise he broke not his fast. Thus devoting himself to mortification and reading for myriads of myriads of years, he won the favour of Kṛishṇa and overcame Death who is so hard to overcome. Brahmā, Bhṛigu, Bhava, Dakṣha, and Brahmā's other sons, men, gods, ancestors, and spirits were exceedingly amazed thereat. Thus observing great vows, with mortification, reading, and disciplines, the saint meditated upon Kṛishṇa with spirit purged of taint. While the saint was thus straining his thought with much effort, there passed away a long time, to wit, six æons. Indra marked this in the seventh æon; he was distrustful of this mortification, and set himself to break it.* He sent to the holy man minstrels and nymphs of heaven, the Love-god, Spring and the breeze of Mount Malaya, Passion and Drunkenness. And these went to his hermitage on the northern slope of the Himalaya, by the river Pushpa-bhadrā and the hill named Chitrā. Pure was his hermitage, pure the trees and climbing plants that adorned it, pure the Brahman families that peopled it, pure and stainless its pools. Wanton bees made music, wanton songbirds warbled, wanton peacocks like pantomimes

* Because, according to Indian ideas, the saint's austerities if continued would give him such merit that he would be able to oust Indra from the throne of the gods. Indra therefore sends temptation to him.

strutted, wanton birds swarmed therein. The breeze as it entered brought with it water-drops from snowy cascades ; as it blew, it was embraced by the flowers, and stirred up Love. Spring appeared there, like the face of Night as the moon arises, in the masses of tender trees and climbing plants putting forth lines of clustered buds. Love showed himself, followed by the minstrels of heaven in singing and playing choirs, bearing his bow and arrows, and leading a troop of celestial damsels. Indra's servants beheld [the saint] worshipping the Fire after sacrifice, his eyes closed, unassailable, like fire in bodily form. The damsels danced before him ; the minstrels sang, and made delightful music with tambours, lutes, and cymbals. Then Love, deeming him conquered, shot his bolt. . . . But all was in vain, like the effort of a powerless man. Scorched by the radiance of the saint whom they were thus assailing, they turned away from him, as children turn on awakening a snake. That the holy man though assailed thus by Indra's servants lapsed not into frailty is not unwonted in noble men. But seeing Love and his troop discomfited, and hearing of the saintly Brahman's majesty, the Lord Indra was sorely amazed.

While the saint was thus straining his thought with mortifications, reading, and disciplines, Hari appeared before him in the form of both

Nara and Nārāyaṇa* to bless him. One of these forms was white, the other swart ; their eyes were like fresh lilies ; four arms had each, and robes of deer-skin and bark ; in their hands were filter-cloths, and each bore a triple scapular, a pitcher, a straight bamboo rod, a lotus, a rosary, an insect-brush, and a bunch of *darbha* grass ; they seemed like the incarnate spirit of Mortification, with a ruddy radiance as of flaming lightning. Tall were they, and worshipped of the chief gods.

Seeing these two forms of the Lord, the holy Nara and Nārāyaṇa, the saint arose reverently, and bent his body like a rod. In the bliss of seeing them his own senses and thought were stilled ; his hair bristling, his eyes full of tears, he could not bear to look upon them. He rose up, and with clasped hands spoke to the Lords lovingly, as if embracing them, the faltering words : "Homage ! homage !" He brought them seats, washed their feet, offered courteous gifts of *arghya*, ointments, perfumes, and garlands. Then when the most venerable Saints were pleasantly seated and disposed to show him grace, he bowed once more at their feet, and spoke thus :

* Two manifestations of Hari (Vishṇu). Nārāyaṇa is the god in his supra-cosmic nature, and represented as dark (or blue) by assimilation to the cult of Kṛishṇa, who is here identified with him ; Nara (literally "man") is the god in human incarnation, especially as the hero Arjuna.

"How can I praise Thee, O Lord, from whose inspiration the breath of life stirs, and in accord with it stir the speech, thought, and senses of bodied beings, of Brahmā and Śiva, and of myself; and withal Thou art kin of spirit to Thy worshippers. These two forms of Thine, O Lord, are for the three worlds' weal, that sorrow may cease and death be overcome; as Thou takest diverse shapes to help the world, so after creating Thou again swallowest up the universe in the manner of a spider. O the feet of this sovereign supporter of moving and unmoving beings! him who stands by them works, moods,* time, and passion affect not, and saints with hearts full of holy lore give them constant praise, reverence, sacrifice, and meditation, that they may win to them! We know, O Lord, no other weal for fear-encompassed man than to take hold of the feet of Thee, who art salvation itself. Brahmā, who holds his seat for two æons, sorely dreads Thy Time-spirit; how much more the beings created by him! I worship the feet of Thee the holy of spirit, the soul's master supreme; by renouncing this profitless, unreal, perishing body and the rest, which veil the soul and are but its

* The "Moods" (*Guṇa*) are the three phases in which, according to Indian theory, primitive Matter manifests itself in finite being. They are (1) *Sattva,* "reality," manifested in brightness, intelligence, and pleasure, (2) *Rajas,* "fieriness," manifested as passion and painful energy, and (3) *Tamas,* "gloom," dulness, dejection, and torpor. See p. 70.

token, man may win of Thee then the full object of desire. The moods of Brightness, Fieriness, and Gloom, causes of the world's continuance, dissolution, and rise, are figures of Thy Magic, under Thy light control, O Lord, friend of the soul. But the mood of Brightness leads to peace; not so the others, whence come to men disaster, frenzy, and dread. Therefore, O Master, as the wise sons of Light * worship the beloved white form of Thee in the spirit and Thee in the flesh,† they deem Brightness to be the Supreme's form, for thence come heaven, fearlessness, joy of soul, and naught else. Homage to the Lord, the Supreme, the Infinite, the Universal, the universe's Master, the deity on high, Nārāyaṇa and saintly supreme Nara, the Swan, stilled of speech, the scriptures' lord! The man with spirit erring in the false paths of sense knows Him not, though He is in his organs, breath, heart, ranges of sense, for His magic darkens the thought; yet that same man, if he win to the lore of Thee, the universe's Master, seeth Thee manifest. I worship Thee, of whom a vision revealing Thy mysteries is seen in the Scripture, for whom bards bond to Brahmā strive in vain, whose nature conforms to

* I have rendered by "sons of Light" the word *Sātvata* in order to keep the word-play on *sattva*, "brightness." Really it means "followers of Satvat," an ancient Vishṇuite sect.

† As manifested respectively as Nārāyaṇa and Nara. The Sanskrit has simply "form of Thee and of Thine."

all descriptions, Supreme Spirit, who art knowledge hidden in personality."

Praised thus by the wise Mārkaṇḍeya of Bhṛigu's race, the Lord Nārāyaṇa together with Nara was pleased, and said: "O worthiest Brahman sage, thou art consummate by rapt meditation upon the soul, by unchanging faith in me, by mortification, reading, and disciplines. We rejoice in thee for thine observance of great vows. Claim what boon thou desirest from the Lord of Boon-givers, and fair fall thee."

The sage said: "Victory to Thee, supreme lord of gods, Achyuta, healer of suppliants' sorrow. Boon enough it is for me to have seen Thee. Thou, of whose blest feet-lilies Brahmā and his company gain sight only in thought ripened by mystic efforts, hast appeared before mine eyes. But I am fain, O thou of eyes like lily-petals, crest-jewel of the blessedly glorious, to look upon the Magic through which the world with its guardian gods imagines a distinction in being." *

Thus worshipped and adored to his pleasure by the holy man, the Lord smiling said, "Be it so!" and then went away to the hermitage of Badarī. And the saint dwelt in his hermitage pondering upon that same thing which is in fire, sun, moon, water, earth, wind, sky, and soul,

* The revelation of Māyā in the form of a universe.

meditating upon Hari, and bringing offerings of spiritual substance. Sometimes, swept away by the tide of love, he even forgot to make offering.

One evening, as he sat in prayer on the bank of the Pushpa-bhadrā, a great wind arose. After this howling and raging wind came awful clouds, which amidst lightning and thunder poured forth from on high rain-drops big as axles of carts. Then the four oceans were seen swallowing up the face of the earth on all sides with billows raised by the winds' fury, amidst the deep roaring of awful sea-monsters and terrible whirlpools. The saint beheld the world in its four classes, together with himself, racked within and without by the waters poured from the heavens, the rude blasts, and the lightnings; he saw the earth flooded; and his heart failed him, and he became afraid. Before his eyes the great Ocean, grim with billows, its floods torn up by the storm, swollen from the raining clouds, swallowed up the very earth with its continents, regions, and mountains. The three worlds, with the earth, atmosphere, heaven, stars, and all the points of space, were flooded. The saint was left alone, and he wandered about with hair flung loose, as though he were mad or blind. Vexed by hunger and thirst, assailed by sea-monsters, beaten by waves and winds, plunged into boundless darkness, overcome by weariness, he wandered without knowing the points of space, or heaven, or earth. Sometimes he came into a great whirlpool, sometimes was lashed by the billows, sometimes was devoured by sea-monsters warring one against another. He suffered ofttimes sorrow, sometimes madness, ofttimes pain, pleasure, or dread, ofttimes even death from the anguish of sickness and the like.

A hundred thousand myriads of myriads of years passed away while he wandered there with spirit darkened by Vishṇu's magic. But one day as he was straying there, the Brahman beheld on a peak of the earth a young fig-tree * bright with fruit and leaves. On a branch thereof that looked to the north-east he saw a babe lying in the hollow of a leaf, consuming the gloom with his radiance. He had the dark hue of noble emeralds, and lovely was his lotus-face ; his neck was like a shell, his breast broad, his nose fine, his brows beauteous. He was adorned with curls that quivered to his breathing, and pomegranate flowers were in his ears, which had the beauty of shells ; the ambrosial whiteness of his smile was touched with redness from the gleam of his coral lips. The corners of his eyes were pink as inner petals of the lotus, and he looked around him with a charming smile. His belly was like an *aśvattha* * leaf, with deep navel quivering in dimpled lines that trembled as he breathed. He drew up his

* *Nyagrodha*, the *Ficus indica.*

lotus-foot with his lovely-fingered hands, put it into his mouth, and sucked it; and the noble Brahman marvelled to see him. At the sight thereof his weariness passed away; in his joy the lotus of his heart and the lilies of his eyes burst into blossom, his hair bristled; but doubting of this wondrous matter, he drew near to the child to question him.

Then the child drew a breath, and Mārkaṇḍeya * like a gnat passed into his body. And he beheld lying therein the universe in its fulness, as it was before; and he was sorely amazed and troubled. He saw atmosphere, heaven and earth, stars, mountains, seas, continents with their regions, the points of space, gods and demons, forests, lands, rivers, towns, mines, villages, herd-folds, the course of life in the Brahman orders and the castes, the primary elements of nature and material things thence sprung, Time that frames the divers æons and ages, and all else that makes for life, displayed as though real; he beheld the Himalaya, the river Pushpavahā, his own hermitage and the holy men there.

As he gazed upon the universe, the child's breath cast him out, and he fell into the ocean of the dissolving world. He saw again the fig-tree growing on the peak of the earth, and the babe lying in the hollow of the leaf, who was

* The *Ficus religiosa*.

gazing upon him with glances beaming with the ambrosia of love. Then as his eyes fell upon the child, whose image was stamped on his heart, he drew near in exceeding distress to embrace him ; for the child was Kṛishṇa. But at once the Lord, manifest Master of the Yoga and Dweller in Mystery, vanished away before the holy man, like a desire framed by the powerless ; and with him straightway disappeared the fig-tree, the waters and universal flood. And Mārkaṇḍeya sat as aforetime in his own hermitage.

XVI. THE WORSHIP OF ŚIVA IN THE SOUTH

As Vishṇu in one or another form is the favourite deity of the Aryan North, so Śiva is the chief god of the Dravidian South. Śiva, "the gracious," appears first as a god of the stormy northern highlands, then as the divine wizard of the hills, a pallid naked Yogi brooding in still millennial ecstasies, or wandering about with his troops of hideous goblins, and at length is recognised as representing the totality of the destructive forces in nature. It is a conception full of horror ; but the Hindu applies neither the æsthetic nor the ethical criteria of ordinary life to his gods, and in the south Śiva has been since immemorial times worshipped with extraordinary affection. He is there truly a national god, a deity dwelling in the hearts of the people. A legend will illustrate this feeling.

In a mountain forest was a rough stone image of Śiva. Every morning a pure and learned Brahman came to it, besprinkled it with holy water, presented proper flowers, and chanted scriptural texts. By chance a young chieftain of a tribe of wild hunters came there one day. At the sight of the image of the unknown god, a great tenderness came upon him. He worshipped it in barbarian fashion, offering wild swine's flesh and jungle flowers, bringing water in his mouth to besprinkle it, and watching by it until dawn. When he had gone, the Brahman arrived. The holy place was, in his eyes, foully polluted ; but he cleansed it as best he could, offered his worship, and departed. The next day the same thing happened, and many other days likewise. One night Śiva appeared in a vision to the Brahman, and revealed all to him. He told him that the savage's formally unclean worship, springing from true devotion, was as acceptable as the purest form of ceremony, and he promised to show the proof. The next day the Brahman concealed himself near the idol, and waited. When the barbarian came to worship, blood began to drip from an eye of the image. The barbarian vainly tried to stanch it. Then he remembered a saying that eye heals eye ; at once he cut out one of his own eyes, and laid it on the idol's eye. The blood ceased to flow from it. But soon the other eye of the idol began to drip blood. At once the barbarian prepared to sacrifice his other eye ; but before he could strike it, the image grasped his hand and the god's voice was heard. He was healed, and henceforth was known as *Kaṇṇappar*, the " Father of the Eye," one of the chosen saints of Siva.

XVII. SIVAITE THEOLOGY IN THE SOUTH

THIS religion of the South has a theology of its own, contained in a luxuriant Tamil literature. This is the *Śaiva-siddhāntam*, or " Sivaite Doctrine." One of the chief bases of this philosophy is a series of Sanskrit Aphorisms, purporting to be a part of the *Raurava-āgama*. A free Tamil paraphrase of these, styled *Śiva-ñāna-bōdham*, was made by the famous divine Mey-kaṇḍa Dēvar about the year 1223, and forms one of the chief textbooks of the school. The Sanskrit verses are to the following effect :

" Since the universe exists in the forms of sex—male, female, and neuter—and is therefore manifestly the work of an efficient cause, it has a

Creator; this is the Lord Hara,* who dissolves and creates it again."

"He is entirely one with our souls, yet other than they; He creates [finite experiences for them] according to their works, making their ways of life by the Power in implicit union with Himself." †

"[The soul] is an infinitely fine substance within the body; for it says *nay, nay*! ‡ it arrogates to itself possession, it is awake when the eyes slumber, it has no enjoyment during sleep, it is the thinker in waking thought."

"It is different from the physical sensorium, although it is associated with it, as a king with his minister. It must exist in five conditions,§ and the energy of its native vision is obstructed by defilement." ||

* Hara means "destroyer." Śiva represents the forces of destruction, as Vishṇu typifies the powers making for constancy and continuance in nature.

† This is the *Śakti* or Divine Grace by which the transcendental Supreme is active in the finite world. It is typified as His bride, and though distinct from Him is connected with Him in *samavāya* union, as *e.g.* the part with the whole.

‡ The soul is conscious of its difference from the material world.

§ These are the states of (1) *waking*, when the soul is supposed to be in the forehead, (2) *dreaming sleep*, when it is in the throat, (3) *dreamless sleep*, when it is in the heart, (4) the "Fourth state," or universal waking consciousness, when it is in the navel, (5) the "state beyond the Fourth," when it is at the base of the spinal cord.

|| See below, p. 80

"The eyes behold the objects of human senses, the soul itself is beheld by the Blessed One. Śiva draws it as the magnet draws the iron, whilst He is immobile."

"Since the invisible is unreal and the visible is brute matter, the form of the Blessed One, as the sages know, must be conceived as different from both."*

"In the presence of Thought, Not-Thought exists not; the twain cannot look one upon the other.† The Soul, which is the knower of the material world and of Śiva, is different from both [the world and Śiva]."

"When the Master admonishes a blest mortal, telling him that from long dwelling amidst the barbarian Senses he knows not his own Soul, the mortal abandons these [Senses], and being now not other [than Śiva], he reaches His feet."

"Seeing with the vision of Thought the Lord in the Soul, abandoning the mirage of finite activity, abiding in the shadow of Śiva's feet, the sage will ponder upon the Five Syllables."‡

"When it has won to union with Śiva, the con-

* Siva Himself is real, *sat*, and immaterial, or of the substance of thought, *chit*.

† At the coming of the Real (Thought), the [relatively] Unreal (Matter) vanishes in it, as darkness, though a relative reality when by itself, vanishes in the higher reality of light.

‡ The *panchāksharī* or mystic formula *Namaś Śivāya*, "Homage to Śiva!"

summated Soul is bond to Him; it makes its actions His, and is untouched by defilement or illusion and the like, being conscious of itself [as one with Him]."

"The Soul gives sight to the eyes; he who gives sight to the Soul is Śiva; therefore one should worship in supreme love Him who does kindness to the Soul."

"In order to salvation one should approach the righteous and worship their form and the temple; thus shall he understand the exposition of Śivaite doctrine in the Perception of the Knowledge of Śiva."

The philosophy of this school is thus obviously very closely akin to that of Rāmānuja. It asserts a trinity, poetically styled *Pati-paśu-pāśam*. The *Pati* or "lord" is the Supreme Śiva, infinitely great in the properties of love, beauty, goodness, power, etc. The *Paśu* or "flock" are the individual finite souls, which are eternally different from Him, and imprisoned in the *pāśam* or "fetter," viz. ignorance (*āṇavam*), the illusive conception of an apparently real world (*māyā*), and *karma*, the accumulation of merit and demerit from previous birth. These are the three "defilements" (*malam*). The Soul in its primordial condition lies in an agony of utter unconsciousness, overwhelmed by the fetter of *āṇavam*. But God in his grace wills that it shall be redeemed and shall dwell in blessedness for ever with Him, in a union not of unity but of perfect association; and therefore the Soul must be born in Man, in order that through human experience salvation may come. Then, when merits have balanced demerits, the defilements of *māyā* and *karma*, which have attached themselves to it in its human incarnation, are taken away by the divine Grace, and the Soul is gathered into the bosom of the infinite Love.

Another little manual of the same school, the *Tiruv-aruḷ-payan* or "Blest Fruit of Grace," written by Umāpati about 1300 A.D., thus teaches in its sixth chapter the way of the soul's enlightenment:

"The body lives by union with the soul; so the embodied soul itself lives by union with the pure Thought."

"As by the sun crystal is made to display its own hue and many other hues, so the earth shows its King's hue." *

"The path of vision is easy; but unless there be a light between eye and soul, there is no vision."

"Conceive thine own work as the Lord's

* The Divine Thought or Grace (like the later Jewish "Wisdom"), as distinct from the Divine Being, is the vivifying force in the universe. It makes the embodied soul conscious of the world and of its God, as in the sunlight the crystal appears both colourless and many-coloured.

work, like unto the workings of the senses which act in menial service."

"Search not, rest thine imagination upon naught, see not with thyself in the foreground. See That which seeth thee." *

"Think of that bliss as a great sense-experience, and hide thyself in the light of the knowledge from all other light."

"See as thou hast seen, see not the not-seeing †; as thou hast been taken, so abide."

XVIII. TWO TAMIL VOTARIES OF ŚIVA

It is however as a religion, rather than as a philosophy, that the Tamil Śivaite school is most remarkable. No cult in the world has produced a richer devotional literature, or one more instinct with brilliance of imagination, fervour of feeling, and grace of expression. Of its many great poets the greatest is Māṇikkavāchakar, or "He of the Ruby Words." ‡ No

* Abandon finite conceptions, ideas based upon empirical thought, and the notion of an *ego*; conceive only of an infinite Grace and Wisdom everywhere surrounding you.

† Accept the revelation of Grace in the form in which it is made to you, and do not sink into the blindness of ignorance.

‡ A recent critic (*Madras Christian College Magazine*, June, 1905) assigns the date of this poet to the eleventh century, or a little earlier.

translation can do full justice to the lyric splendour of his style; but a short quotation from his *Tiru-vāchakam*, the "Blest Utterance," will perhaps indicate something of its character.

O barrer of ways of beguiling sense, who wellest forth in my heart,
Pure fount of nectar, O Light Supreme, shew Thyself unto me as Thou art.
Of Thy grace appear, Thou clearest of clear, whose home is the Mighty Shrine,
Thou Bliss transcending all states unending, O perfect Love that is mine!

With love Thy minion's body and soul are melting in rapture away;
Thou gavest me grace beyond my power—and I have naught to repay.
Outspread All-before and All-after, of yore first, boundless in freedom divine,
Lord Śiva, King of fair Śiva-town, whose home is the Southland Shrine!

King, Father to me who am least in the band of thy lovers, O Radiance of Truth,
Who hast melted with bliss all my body and soul, and banished the gloom of unsooth,
Thought thinking what passeth the speech and the thought, bright billowless Nectar-sea,
O thou whose home is the Southland Shrine, now teach me fit greeting to Thee!

Thou Fulness consummate, pure Nectar of bliss, Mount rising in limitless fire,
Who camest to stay in my heart alway as the Vedas and Vedas' desire,

Didst stream in my soul as a swelling flood, bound-bursting
with hurtling wave,
Thine abode hast Thou made in my body to-day; what
more of Thy grace can I crave?

O Splendour dawning within my soul as I sink in swooning
desire,
Whose lotus-feet ruddily deck the crowns of the chiefs of
the heavenly choir,
Who art all-spread Ether, Earth, Water, Air, Fire—who
art these, yet other than they—
Whose shape in their shape is hidden—O joy, to have seen
Thy vision to-day!

The darkness to-day Thou dravest away, didst dawn in my
heart as the sun.
In thought beyond thought my spirit hath sought Thy being:
save Thee there is none.
Thou art One, art the Energy stirred for aye, self-subliming
to endless degree;
Thou art other than aught; save Thee there is naught—Oh,
who may have knowledge of Thee?

Outspreading in single expanse of light, Thy blossom the
earth and the spheres,
Fire water-laden, pure dweller for aye in being which thought
not nears,
O Sweetness welling within the heart by the flood of Thy
mercy made bright,
Here who is my kindred, and who is not? Oh, bliss-giving
heavenly Light!

Thou gavest Thyself, and me didst take; wert Thou the
more cunning, or I?
I got of Thee bliss everlasting, O Thou whose home is in
Perun-durai;

From me what hast Thou won, my Sovran? for Thou hast made of my spirit Thy fane,
And hast set Thine abode in my body to-day—all mine the unrecompensed gain! *

Similar in thought, but even more mystical in expression, is the "Revel in Bliss" of Tāyumānavar, a poet who flourished about the beginning of the eighteenth century, in which the Soul tells in ballad form of the visit of her divine Lover.

"The Light which is the beginning and hath no beginning, which shineth in me as Bliss and Thought, appeared as the Silent One.† He spake to me, sister, words not to be spoken."

"The words that were spoken, how shall I tell? Cunningly He seated me all alone, with nothing before me. He made me happy, beloved, he grasped me and clung to me."

"He bade me put all other clingings aside, and cling to Him within. What I got as I clung to Him, how shall I tell? He spake of things never spoken, beloved."

"I had wandered about, babbling, telling of

* For the above version I must acknowledge my debt for several turns of phrase to the translation by Mr. Arunachalam, from whom I have also borrowed, with some modifications, the prose rendering of the following poem.

† *Mauni*, an epithet of Śiva, as being absorbed in millennial reverie; Mauna Guru is also the name of the poet's teacher. Compare note on p. 56.

untold woes, a mere devil-ridden body. But the Lord drove away the demon of desire, and held me down at His feet, beloved."

"Holding down, withdrawing the senses, I gathered love for His form. He folded me unto Himself, sister, and blended with me so that I could not speak at all."...

"'Whatsoever thy heart hitherto hath looked upon in its thought as real and unreal, cast away,' said my Lord, and He made me Himself. Behold His cunning, sister."

"'The earthly and other elements thou art not; reflect—the earthly organs of action and sense thou art not. Thou art pondering Thought.' Blissful are the words that the Lord spoke in love, sister."

"To His lovers He is love, He is true, my Lord. The blissful Silent One, the gracious Master, laid His foot on my head. Lo, I knew myself. I died to sense."

"I considered how death and birth came to be companions to me. They grew, beloved, from the treacherous illusive Sense which is alike oblivion and thought."

"O Sense, was it not for me that God came under the stone-banyan tree as the Silent Teacher, and with dumb show of hand annulled the works that were mine, and set me in the blissful ocean of His Grace?"

"'By Grace behold everything!' he said.

I had beheld with my understanding in conceptions without understanding; I saw naught but darkness, saw not even myself the seer. What is this, sister?"

"'Think not in thy heart of Me as other than thee; be thou without second.' When He uttered this one word, how can I tell the bliss that grew from that Word?"

"The field where grew the bliss of Śiva, that pure space I drew near. Weeding out the weeds of darkness, I then looked. Save the Lord's splendour, I saw naught, sister."

"Life, the laughing-stock of all that see, with both our eyes we see depart; it passeth away as in sleep. Say, what good, what merit, is there in it, sister?"

"To me who knew naught of good, He granted the search for the pure Stillness that is beyond the Sound.* He rid me of all unrest, the all-powerful One, with His foot He struck my head, sister."

"The blessed Light of Bliss that struck me by His grace made me, who am less than an atom, into perfect Fulness without motion hither or thither. Lo, the strangeness of it, sister!"

"Making, maintaining, destroying—all these are the works of the Almighty, yet they

* *Nādam,* the first (or male principle) infinite being, born of Śiva and his Grace.

touch Him not, not so much as a grain of sesame. On this true Witness it is well to think, sister."

"There Thought is born, there Thought dieth away and is purified; there all states are; there I who see am standing without second."

"Is there a 'there' or a 'here' when the glory of the Trinity of Being, Thought, and Bliss hath been seen arising and spreading abroad in undivided manifestation? Can we spea then of *one* or *two*?" . . .

"Is there a Yea and a Nay? If thou wouldst have bliss, thou wilt know it by abiding awhile as Understanding; thus is the mystic rule that our Lord spake, sister."

XIX. ŞIVAITE PURITANS

MĀṆIKKA-VĀCHAKAR is the favourite poet of the orthodox Şivaite church. Its rites inspired many of his hymns, and he has found his reward in being sung in numberless temples. But it is not so with all the votaries of this school. Their mystic faith often led them into conflict with the formal ritualism of the established church. One of the most notable of these unorthodox saints was Paṭṭaṇattu Piḷḷai, who is believed to have flourished some ten centuries ago. Among his numerous poems is one which runs as follows : *

My God is not a chiselled stone
  Or lime-block clear and bright,
No bronzen image He, forsooth,
  That's cleansed with tamarind.

I cannot worship such as these,
  But make my lofty boast
That in my heart I set the feet,
  The golden feet of God.

If He be mine, what can I need ?
  My God is everywhere.
Within, beyond man's highest word,
  My God abideth still.

In sacred books, in darkest night,
  In deepest, bluest sky,
In those who know the truth, and in
  The faithful few on earth ;—

My God is found in all of these ;
  But can the Deity
Descend to images of stone
  Or copper dark and red ?

Where'er wind blows or compass points,
  God's light doth stream and shine.
Yet see yon fool—beneath his arm
  He bears the sacred roll.

* The following poems of Paṭṭaṇattu Piḷḷai and Śivavākyar are given in the version of Mr. Gover (*Folk-songs of Southern India*), with some slight modifications.

How carefully he folds the page
  And draws the closing string!
See how he binds the living book,
  That not a leaf escape!

Ah, yes! the truth should fill his heart;
  But 'tis beneath his arm.
To him who knows, the sun is high;
  To this, 'tis starless night.

If still, O sinful man, with ash *
  Thou dost besmear thy face,
Or bathest oft, that thus thy soul
  May cast away its load,

Thou knowest naught of God, nor of
  Regeneration's work.
Your *mantras*,† what are they? The Veds
  Are burdened with their weight.

If knowledge be not thine, thou art
  As one in deep midstream,
A stream so wide that both the banks
  Are hidden from thine eyes.

Alas! how long did I adore
  The chiselled stone, and serve
An image made of lime or brass
  That's cleansed with tamarind!

Many verses of the same nature are to be found in the collection of poems known as *Siva-vākyam*,

* The Śivaite votaries smear themselves with the ash of burnt cow-dung.

† The sacred verses from the Vedas used in rituals.

" Śiva-speeches." The nucleus of the *Śiva-vākyam* was seemingly the work of a poet or poets of the same monotheistic and unorthodox school as Paṭṭaṇattu Piḷḷai ; but orthodox editors have greatly garbled the book by inserting as a corrective to this heresy verses more to their own taste. Thus " Śiva-vākyar," as the supposed author of the whole collection is styled, is as incongruous as the Sphinx—in one verse a gross idolator, in another an exalted worshipper of One God. As examples of the latter vein we quote a few stanzas :

When once I knew the Lord,
What were to me the host
Of pagan deities,
Some fixed in temple shrines,
Or carried in the crowd ;
Some made of unbaked clay,
And some burnt hard with fire ?
With all the lying tales
That fill the sacred books,
They've vanished from my mind.

How many flowers I gave
At famous temple-shrines !
How often told my bede
And washed the idols' head !
And still with weary feet
Encircled Śiva's shrines !
But now at last I know
Where dwells the King of Gods,
And never will adore
A temple made by hands.

But yet I have a shrine—
The mind within my breast.
An image too is there—
The soul that came from God.
I offer ash and flowers—
The praises of my heart;
And all the God-made world
Is frankincense and myrrh.
And thus where'er I go
I ever worship God.

Yet two more stanzas from this strange book may be quoted before we leave it—stanzas such that the inexperienced reader is tempted to wonder whether "Śiva-vākyar" was not a worshipper at the local Christian church:

When Thou didst make me, Thou didst know my all:
But I knew not of Thee. 'Twas not till light
From Thee brought understanding of Thy ways
That I could know. But now where'er I sit,
Or walk, or stand, Thou art for ever near.
Can I forget Thee? Thou art mine, and I
Am only Thine. E'en with these eyes I see,
And with my heart perceive, that Thou art come
To me as lightning from the lowering sky.

If thy poor heart but choose the better part,
And in this path doth worship only God,
His heart will stoop to thine, will take it up
And make it His. One heart shall serve for both.

XX. "KAPILAR" AND THE ANTI-BRAHMANS

THE South of India is one of the most interesting corners of the world; and one of the most curious features in it is its mixed culture. Its inhabitants are for the most part Dravidians, entirely distinct in blood and speech from the Aryan tribes who entered the North-West of India more than a thousand years before Christ, bringing with them a culture and tongue akin to those of Europe and the rudiments of the Brahmanic religion which has in course of time assimilated nearly all the older worships of the land. The Dravidians had even in those ancient days a civilisation of their own, which was not inferior to that of the Aryans. The influences of Aryan conquest, of Brahmanic religion, and of Sanskritic literature have greatly obscured the traces of this old Dravidian culture and religion, and in many cases have entirely obliterated them. But the spirit of the olden days is still manifest in many places, and nowhere more than in the popular poetry of the South.

The Brahmans in many parts of Southern India hold a position like that of the Normans in Plantagenet England. They are there by right of political or religious conquest; but they have generally assimilated themselves to local conditions, and developed their own religious and social institutions in accordance with those that are native to the South. Many of them have been, and many are still, men of high intellect and noble character; and much of the finest literature of India is the work of Southern Brahmans.* But withal they remain in a sense foreigners; and to the first principle of their creed, the arrangement of society in castes under the semi-divine presidency of the Brahman, the Dravidian people has never fully assented. Two popular works typically express this antagonism. One is Tamil, the *Agaval* of Kapilar; the other is Telugu, the *Padyamulu* of Vēmana.

We have already seen that Rāmānanda and the other Vishṇuite reformers of his school vigorously preached the religious brotherhood of man. But the Dravidian protestants were many centuries earlier in the field. Like the Buddhists and Jains, they boldly attacked the whole structure of the Brahmanic caste-system, and, to clinch their protest by the *argumentum ad hominem*, they satirically contrasted the high spiritual pretensions of the Brahmans with the low standard of the lives of many of them. Their

* To mention only a few of the greatest names, Śankara, Rāmānuja, Ánanda-tīrtha, and Sāyaṇa, the great commentator on the Vedas, were Brahmans of the South.

words found echoes in the heart of the people. The verses current under the name of Vēmana are the most cherished folk-poetry of the Telugus; and the *Agaval* has become a Tamil classic.

Of Kapilar himself a folk-story is told. In the Chola country there lived a Brahman who went on a pilgrimage to the river Ganges, and did not return. He left a young son, Bhagavan by name, who when he grew to manhood set out in search of his father. As he sat in a rest-house near Melur, cooking a meal, a low-caste little girl, who had been found in the road and adopted by the kindly owner of the rest-house, approached him. Her presence was a defilement to his Brahmanship; he drove her away, throwing a spoon—or a stone, according to some accounts—which wounded her on the head. After some years Bhagavan came back to the same place; his quest had been vain. The child was now a beautiful woman; Bhagavan, not recognising her, fell in love and married her. On the fifth day of the wedding ceremonies, as he parted her hair in order to pour oil upon it, he saw the scar of the wound that he had inflicted years before. His memory returned; she was *Ādi-āḷ*, "the First woman," the girl whom he had met long ago. Horrified at the thought of his past and present deeds, he fled away. But Ādi was not minded to be cheated out of her husband; she ran after him, and caught him. Thereupon he promised to take her with him as his wife, but on the hard condition that she should abandon every child whom she should bear. She gave birth to four daughters, Uppai, Auvai, Uṟuvai, and Vaḷḷi, and to three sons, Adhikamān, Tiru-vaḷḷuvar, and Kapilar; and in every case she kept the cruel compact with Bhagavan. But each babe, as she sorrowfully left it, comforted her by uttering a verse telling of the Providence which cares for all. The fate of these children we shall learn from "Kapilar" himself. Their verses are still preserved; I quote those ascribed to Uppai, Uṟuvai, and Vaḷḷi *:

Shall Nāri's † lord the rain command
  And dew to feed the thorny trees
Which in the dismal forest stand,
  Where eye of mortal never sees,
And not my daily food supply,
But leave his votary to die?

The lively chick that breaks the shell
  May guardian grace and power attest,
And nourished infancy dispel
  The doubts that tear thy troubled breast.
In Aran's ‡ name of truth and power
Find firmness for the evil hour.

* These are given in the translation of Mr. E. J. Robinson.
† Nāri is Umā or Pārvatī, the wife of the god Śiva.
‡ *Aran* is Tamil for *Hara*, a title of Śiva.

Whose head the serpent's gleams adorn,
Who dances at the Veda's end,
Who cherished me when yet unborn,
Will Perumān * not still befriend ?
The future's written in the past :
His providence must ever last.

This tale is an example of the way in which a mass of legend gathers around the slenderest nucleus of fact. It is quite possible that there was a poet named Kapilar—the word is Sanskrit, and means "tawny"—and that he composed the *Agaval*, and perhaps also the other classical verses ascribed to him ; it may be likewise that his bitterness against the Brahmanic caste-system arose because he himself was a half-caste Brahman and was denied the rank of his father, and perhaps also had seen his mother hardly used. The aristocrat's bastard often becomes a dangerous democrat. But even this is guess-work. The names, on the other hand, are redolent of myth. *Kapila* is the title given in the *Śvetā-śvatara Upanishad* (verse 2) to the Demiurge or World-spirit, who is the first emanation of the Primal Being, Brahma, whom the Tamils call by the Sanskrit epithet *Ādi-bhagavan*, "The First Lord" ; and it seems fairly clear that the names of the legendary Kapilar's father and mother, Ādi and Bhagavan, are simply inventions of ignorant story-tellers to explain the fact that

* Another epithet of Śiva, meaning "the Lord."

Kapilar was called the son of Ādi-bhagavan.* Seemingly then a god known as Kapilar and a real but nameless poet, of whom possibly a few verses survived, were mixed up in legend, and the present folk-tale was thus formed, upon which the poem was based.

But the farrago of fact and fancy includes other names, which are also instructive. The seven children of Adi and Bhagavan comprise three daughters—Uppai, Uṟuvai, and Vaḷḷi—who are local goddesses in the Tamil land; of them and of their brother Adhikamān practically nothing more is known than the story given above. On the other hand, Auvai is the name of an ancient poetess to whom are ascribed several popular moral poems much used in schools; and Tiru-vaḷḷuvar is the title of the nameless writer of the *Kuṟaḷ*, the great collection of ethical verses which is perhaps the best-loved book in the Tamil language. The evidence for the common parentage of these authors and deities is merely the folk-tale, which has made brothers and sisters of a number of partly real and partly mythical persons, who previously had few or no common links. Local gods are often foundlings, like Romulus and Remus;

* A fact that strongly supports this view is that in some versions of the legend Bhagavan is actually the grandson of Brahma. Compare Aśvaghosha's *Buddha-charita*, xii. 12, identifying the legendary philosopher Kapila with Prajāpati.

and when folk-tale has no information as to the parentage of popular authors such as Auvai or Tiru-vaḷḷuvar, it is prone to justify its ignorance by turning them into foundlings likewise.

From this digression we turn to " Kapilar " and his criticisms of the Brahmans.

Our poet begins by asking a long list of questions upon the origin of the world and the principles of nature, by way of showing his disbelief in the glib answers to these problems given by the Brahman pandits ; and then he turns to his main theme, the supreme importance of good works, with furious energy :

" O folk of the world, folk of the world, hearken, hearken to what I proclaim with beat of the drum of my mouth by the stick of my tongue. The term of man's life is but an hundred years ; fifty glide away in sleep, five more are spent in childhood, then thrice five are spent in youth, and now that seventy have passed there remain but thrice ten. Few are these days of joy, few these days of sorrow ; thus wealth is like a swollen river, youth like the crumbling bank of a swollen river, life like a tree on the crumbling bank. Then do the one thing, the one that is needed—do good, for good is needed ; do it to-day, for to-day is needed. If ye shall say " to-morrow, to-morrow ! " ye know not what is your term of life. Whenever it may be that the Death-god cometh, when he doth come he will have naught of your worship of him, naught of your wealth, naught of your proffers, naught of your kindred. He recketh not whether one be good or poor, whether evil or rich. Fierce of eye, he halteth not for a moment ; he taketh away the soul, and will have naught of the body. O ye hapless mortals who mourn, is it the spirit or the body that is lost ? Do ye aver that the spirit is lost ? But ye cannot behold it even to-day apart from the body. Is it the body that is lost ? But ye tie that very body hand and foot, like a thief who has stolen, strip it of its clothing, fasten on it a loin-cloth, kindle a high-mounting funeral fire, and burn it until it becometh ash, then ye dip yourselves in the stream, and go away with your folks, grieved in soul. Is this to be called a pretence, or a play ? Ye Brahmans, hearken to what I say ! When men die and their sons give you a seat and food so that you recite delusive catch-prayers and enjoy yourselves, tell me, who has ever seen [the ghosts], stirred by hunger, come back and stand there thrusting out their hands ? whose hunger is assuaged by the food that you consume ! In the various lands of the Oṭṭiyas, Mlechchhas, Hūṇas, Sinhalese, the slender-waisted Jonakas, Yavanas, and Chinese there are no Brahmans ; but ye have set up in this land a fourfold caste-division as if it were an order distinguished in primal nature. By conduct are distinguished high and low degrees. The bull and the buffalo are unlike of kind; have male and female of these two classes ever been seen to unite one with another and breed offspring? But ye men, who are by birth all of the same kind, do ye not see that if male and female of the orders which ye proclaim to be different unite one with another, offspring is born from the union? Whatever be the seed and whatever the ground whereon it is sown, on that same ground that very seed will spring up; it would be against nature's law that it should become different. Are not the sons born of a Pulai-woman united with a Brahman likewise Brahmans? Who can see any unlikeness of form between men such as there is between bull and buffalo? In our life, our limbs, our body, hue, and understanding no difference is revealed. A Pulai-man of the south-land who should go to the north and unflaggingly study will be a Brahman; a Brahman of the north-land who should come to the south and be warped in his ways will be a Pulai-man. Vasishṭha, born of a lowly mistress to Brahmā, like a red water-lily springing up in mire; Śakti, born of a Chaṇḍāla woman to Vasishṭha; Parāśara, born to Śakti of a Pulai-woman; Vyāsa, born of a fisher-girl to Parāśara,—all these by study of the Vedas rose to high estate and are famous as holy men. I, Kapilar, with them that were born with me, who are the lineal offspring born to the austere and saintly Bhagavan by the good Pulai-lady Ādi of the great town of Karuvūr,—we are in number three males and four females; and hearken to the brief tale of our nurture. Uppai grew up as a dweller in a Vaṇṇār * household at Ūṭṭukāḍu town. Uṟuvai was reared in the home of Śānārs, in the toddy-drawers' village at Kāviri-pumbaṭṭiṇam. Auvai was reared in the home of Pāṇars, in the village belonging to the viol-players. Vaḷḷi grew up on the fair mountain-side where the lordly Kuṟavars gather their teeming crops. Vaḷḷuvar was nurtured among the pariahs of pleasant Mailapur in the Toṇḍai-maṇḍalam. Adhikamān was reared with a chieftain of Vanji, where blossom the tree-groves and bees swarm. I grew up nurtured by Brahmans in Ārūr, the land of gushing streams."

"Doth the rain in its descent avoid certain men, or doth the wind as it bloweth leave aside certain? Doth the earth refuse to bear their weight, or the sun deny its warmth to certain? Do the four high-born races get their food from the land, and the four base-born races their food from the forest? Fortune and poverty are the fruit of our own deeds, and death is the

* The *Vaṇṇār* are a caste of washermen; the *Sānār* (Shanar) are drawers of toddy-wine from palm-trees; the Pāṇar are musicians.

common lot of all children of earth ; one is their race, one their family, one their death, one their birth, one the God whom they revere. To neglect not the sayings spoken by the men of old, to give alms at all times to suppliants, to eschew vice, bloodshed, and theft, to know how to stand on a sure footing in righteousness, to understand That which is neither male nor female, to be gentle of speech,—this is the blameless life. Can birth, instead of worth and virtue, bring good, fools that ye are ? "

XXI. SOME MORE TAMIL MORALISTS

MORAL poetry is not held in very high esteem by modern Europeans, from a literary point of view. There are two good reasons, if not more. The writers who have essayed ethical themes are as a rule endowed with little technical skill or imagination, and so cannot be read without weariness of soul by a generation that knows Tennyson or Shelley. Moreover, the West has little taste for an abstract moral proposition ; it loves works that appeal to its romantic or its sensuous imagination. Besides, the magnificent force of the Bible's lessons has dulled our ears for all feebler utterances. Hence a cultured

European sitting down in cold blood to write a verse upon virtue is hardly conceivable; another European reading him without yawning is almost wholly unimaginable.

It was otherwise with the ancient Greeks. So long as they remained worthy of their name, they loved their *γνῶμαι*, and honoured the man who could clothe a noble and true thought in vigorous verse. But the East, with its love of meditation and its amazing wealth of literary skill, is the true home of the gnomic poet; and India has a long list of them. Here we may fitly say a few words about two Tamil books, the *Kuṟaḷ* and the *Nāl-aḍiyār*.

Of the *Kuṟaḷ* and its legendary author Tiru-vaḷḷuvar we have already made passing mention.* Really nothing is known of Tiru-vaḷḷuvar. Tradition tells that he was the brother of Kapilar and Auvaiyār, and having been picked up as a foundling by some kindly people was adopted by them, and lived as a pariar priest in Mailai, the modern Mailapur or San Thomé, outside Madras. Even his religion is unknown, so vague is his language when he speaks of it. Some have even thought that Christian influences may have leavened his thought; but this seems more than unlikely. His *Kuṟaḷ* is a collection of tiny verses (hence the name, from *kuṟu*, "short") in three sections treating respectively of virtue,

* See above, p. 102.

polity, and love. It is not a book that can be effectively quoted in a translation, for much of its force depends upon its marvellous pithiness. Thus its opening verse sums up in eight words the Hindu principles both of metaphysics and phonetics :

> Agara mudalav eṛutt' ellām ādi
> bhagavan mudaṯṯē ulagu.

"As all the letters have as their beginning *A*, so the universe has for its beginning the Primal Lord." Here plainly the Italian adage *traduttori traditori* is very applicable. Nevertheless a translation of a few of his apophthegms may raise some interest in a great writer undeservedly ignored by the West.

"Virtue is spotlessness of mind; all else is mere noise."

"He who lives the natural household life does more nobly than any who make extraordinary efforts." *

"What is nobler than woman, if she have the might of purity ?"

"Bowing not before the gods but before her husband, rising up—when she bids the rain fall, it falls." †

* This is an attack upon the Yogis and other ascetics who endeavour to attain salvation by renouncing family ties, mortifying the flesh, and training the mind to abstract meditation.

† This describes the power of the ideal wife.

" 'The flute is sweet, the viol is sweet,' say they who have never heard the prattling of children of their own."

" The body *lives* that is instinct with *love*; the body of such as lack love is but a carcass covered with bone and skin."

" It is not good to forget a good deed; it is good to forget at once deeds not good."

" They who cannot act in harmony with the world, though they may have learned much, understand nothing."

" Duty needs no reward; what can the world do for the rain-cloud?"

" There is naught bitterer than death—yet it is sweet when one has naught to give."

The *Kuṟaḷ* with its genial idealisation of domestic life is in sharp contrast to the *Nālaḍiyār* or "Quatrain-writers," a collection of verses by nameless Jain poets. Here the characteristic sentiment of the Jains, a morbid dislike of the flesh and of even the most innocent domestic attachments, is most powerfully expressed. Witness the following:

" She that was my mother left me here, and went away to seek a mother for herself *; so likewise did her mother. And thus the world goes on its easy way, mother seeking mother."

* Meaning that her soul has departed to become incarnated in another womb.

"The ties of friendship are broken; the kindly are become few; the bonds of love likewise are loosened. Look within! A cry comes up as from a sinking ship: 'What profit hath thy life?'"

"They march, and once strike the drum.* They wait a little while, then strike it again. Lo, 'tis good! When the third beat is struck, they put on the shroud, take fire, and go forth, the doomed bearing the dead."

"In answer to him who sees how they carry forth the dead to the burning-ground amidst the anguished wails of banded kinsfolk, and nevertheless weds and believes that there is aught real here, the drum peals forth, and mockingly gives him the lie." †

"Unseen men come, and are born into the home of kin; and silently they pass away. As the bird forsakes its nest on the tree, and in silence passes away to a far bourn, so do they leave to their kinsmen their body."

For love the *Nāl-aḍiyār* have the bitterest contempt. They dwell with saturnine glee on the frailty and foulness of the body, and bid the lover look upon the loathsome scenes of the graveyard to cure his fitful fever. One of the least morbid of their stanzas asks: "What do

* A description of the funeral procession.

† The onomatopœic word-play of the Tamil is quite untranslatable.

the worthies who babble of a 'mango-hued maiden simple and fair' know of a spiritual abode? Let but a bit of skin as big as a fly's wing be broken off from the body, and a stick is needed to drive off the crows!"

Like most moralists, they have their gibes at Fortune. "Mark how the masters of great and abundant lore fall into want and suffer misery," remarks one; "ay, for since the Lady of the Tongue,* ancient of renown, dwells with them, the Lady of the Flower † is sulky, and approaches them not." Our fates are predetermined by our deeds in former births: "The fortunes ordained in the early time ‡ grow neither less nor greater, nor come in changed order, nor help as a staff in times of stress, but come as they must come; then why sorrow at the hour of dissolution?"

At times a higher note is struck. They plead for charity and righteousness also, and preach the Stoic wisdom. "O heart," cries one of them, "thou forsakest not the fetters of wedded life; how many ages, forsooth, wilt thou live yearning for children? No profit doth the soul gather save the good that it hath done, slight though

* Sarasvati, the goddess of learning and eloquence.

† Lakshmī, the goddess of fortune, who is throned on the lotus.

‡ While the babe is in the womb, or perhaps, according to the popular idea, on the sixth day after birth, when the Creator writes its destiny upon its forehead.

its measure be." "Sow seed for the other world with spirit unconfounded," says another, "and live your life without debasement. As ye stand in your place of wisdom, hues will fade, and many things mysteriously come to pass." For the wise man is the spectator of life, and the heir of eternity.

XXII. VĒMANA

THE Higher Criticism, if it ever falls upon Vēmana, will find in him a ready victim. For though "Vēma" or "Vēmana" is a real Telugu personal name, nothing is known of the writer of the collection of verses which, under the title of "Vēmana's Padyamulu," embody the homely wit, wisdom, philosophy, and religion of the farmers of Telingana. One verse indeed suggests that he was a yeoman; but a Higher Critic, not without plausibility, might reject this evidence and maintain that "Vēmana" is a Telugu "Poor Richard," an imaginary village sage in whose mouth have been placed the verses of a number of nameless rustic poets. Be this as it may, the *Padyamulu* are a most interesting hotch-potch of popular poetry, springing straight from the heart of the sturdy yeomanry of Telingana and racy of the soil.

Vēmana's theology is Śivaite in tone, but simple and tolerant. He cares not for divisions of church and caste, or for sectarian nostrums for procuring salvation. A few of his sayings, gathered at random, will explain his homely creed.*

"He whose form is universal; who is eternal; who Himself witnesses all that passes in every heart, who exists immutably throughout the universe, and is free from all shadow, is called God." "Neither in earth nor metal, wood or stone, painted walls or images, does that great Spirit dwell so as to be perceived."

"We take a skin, and form it into a pretty puppet; we make it play, and then throw it away. But who can see Him who plays with us?"

"Those who roam [to other lands in pilgrimage] to find the God that dwells within them are like a shepherd who searches in his flock for the sheep that he has under his arm."

"'Benares! Benares!' they cry, and delight to travel thither. Yet is not the same God here as there? If thy heart be aright, He is there and here also."

"Kine are of divers colours, but all milk is alike; the kinds of flowers vary, yet all worship

* My quotations are taken from the version of Mr. C. P. Brown, with a few slight verbal alterations.

is one *; systems of faith are different, but the Deity is one."

"If thy heart become calm as the breezeless firmament and the unruffled waveless deep, changeless and unmoving—this is called Salvation."

"What Thou sayest I will say; where Thou dwellest I will remain enrapt; my thoughts shall be like to Thine; and when Thou smilest, I will also smile."

Vēmana has many a scornful and bitter word for the Brahman ritualists and ascetic devotees who set their hopes of salvation upon formal ceremonies.†

"The solitariness of a dog! the meditations of a crane! the chanting of an ass! the bathing of a frog! ‡ Ah, why will ye not try to know your own hearts?"

* Flowers are commonly used as offerings in worship of the gods.

† Of course strictures like those of Vēmana must be accepted with some reserve. The followers of religion in India belong, generally speaking, to one of two great classes, the "beneficed clergy" and the ascetics. The former, who are the officiants in temples and holy places, are usually men of slight culture, and sometimes of lax character. The ascetic orders include a vast number of vagabonds and charlatans, but also many men of learning and high spirituality, who exercise a real "pastoral" influence, whatever be the defects of their theology. Besides these classes there are the orthodox laic Brahmans of high caste who observe the Vedic rituals; they are often men of wide culture and fine character.

‡ Four important ceremonial duties of the Brahmans are here derided.

"Will the application of white ashes do away with the smell of a wine-pot? Will a cord cast over your neck make you twice-born?" *

"What are you the better for smearing your body with ashes? Your thoughts should be set on God alone; for the rest, an ass can wallow in dirt as well as you."

"The books that are called the Vedas are like courtesans, deluding men, and wholly unfathomable; but the hidden knowledge of God is like an honourable wife."

"O ye asses! why do you make balls of food and give them to the crows in the name of your ancestors! how can a dung-eating crow be an ancestor of yours?"

"He that fasts shall become [in his next birth] a village pig; he that embraces poverty shall become a beggar; and he that bows to a stone shall become like a lifeless image."

For caste-divisions he had a noble scorn. "If we carefully observe and examine the universe," he says, "we shall see that all castes have equally arisen therein. Then all are equal; surely all men are brothers." And again he asks: "Why should we constantly revile the Pariar? Are not his flesh and blood the same as our own? And of what caste is He who pervades the Pariar?"

The whole comedy of life, however, has an

* See above, p. 65. The cord is an emblem of the Brahmanic caste.

interest for Vēmana ; like the old gentleman in Terence's play, he is indifferent to nothing human. The lash of his satire falls upon many backs. For the miser he had a lively hatred. "Would you kill a miser," he says, "no poison in the world is needed. There is another way : ask him for a penny, and he will at once fall down dead." And again he remarks : "If a corpse leave a miser's house when he has paid the money for the shroud and bier, 'Alas for the fees !' he cries, sobbing and weeping away." "You may drive out Nature with a pitchfork," said the Latin satirist, "but still she will come back"; and in the same spirit Vēmana says : "If you take a dog's tail and put it into a bamboo tube, it will remain straight only for a while ; say what you will, a bad man will not lose his crooked disposition." And again he writes : "Though he roam to the Konkan, no dog will turn into a lion ; going to Benares will make no pig an elephant ; and no pilgrimage will make a saint of one whose nature is untoward."

He had no great reverence for a Jack-in-office. Perhaps he had in view some local Dogberry when he wrote : "If you catch a monkey and dress it in a new coat, the hill-apes will all worship it. Thus are the luckless subject to the senseless."

The inconsistency of the orthodox was another of his themes. He remarks : "If you see a bull made of marble, you bow down ceremoniously to it; but if you see a trotting bullock, you beat it.* Surely the worshippers of the bull are wretched sinners!"

The following remark is Socratic in its first clause: "He who says 'I know nothing' is the shrewdest of all. He who says 'I am learning' is a mere talker. He who holds his peace is the wisest and best."

Two sayings of Vēmana in particular deserve to be quoted, for they contain thoughts which we are apt to deem our own exclusive possession. The command "Let not thy left hand know what thy right hand doeth"† is worthily echoed by him: "Desert not your king, even for a thousand others; when you have given a man food, tell it not, however poor you are; and however fair the wife be, let her not scorn her husband." And the bidding to heap coals of fire upon an enemy's head by doing kindness to him‡ is likewise repeated by him. "Though a foe worthy of death fall into thy hand," he says, "afflict him not. Conciliate him by kindness, and bid him depart. This is death to him."

These are truly golden words, and the more precious because they spring not from a cloistered

* The worship of cows is common throughout India; but the Śivaites pay especial reverence to the divine bull Nandi, the favourite of Śiva, and hence also to all earthly cattle.

† Matthew, vi. 3.

‡ Proverbs, xxv. 21-2.

virtue but from the toiling, loving heart of the people. When the teachers and preachers of mankind are weighed in the balance by the Searcher of Hearts, many a lofty and glorious spirit will be found of less worth than this humble yeoman of Telingana.

XXIII. BHARTṚI-HARI

In all his many moods Bhartṛi-hari is singularly typical of his nation. The native tradition, probably without good grounds, tells us that he, like the Preacher of Jerusalem, was a king *; and the spirit of the first and the last of his three "Centuries" of Sanskrit verses is often notably akin to that of the Proverbs and Ecclesiastes. His "Century of Morals," the *Nīti-śataka*, embodies the worldly wisdom of ripe manhood. The word *nīti* denotes both political and social ethics. For the former, however, Bhartṛi-hari seems to have had little admiration; he remarks with some bitterness that "the polity of princes—at once truthful and false, rude and courteous of speech, cruel and compassionate, greedy and generous, constantly spending and constantly

* From the account of I-tsing he died about 650 A.D. He was probably the author also of the *Vākya-padīya*, a bulky treatise upon the philosophy of grammar.

drawing rich revenues—is as many-sided as a courtesan." He was intensely interested in the moral life of mankind, paying willing homage to noble ideals, and stoutly castigating baseness and folly. Let him speak for himself.

"The wealth that the Creator has assigned to him in the writing on his forehead,* be it small or great, a man will assuredly find even in a desert, and not more than this will he find on Meru.† Then be brave, and live not a life of vanity and misery among the wealthy; see, the pitcher draws the same quantity of water in the well and in the ocean."

"The wise man's course of life is twofold, like that of the flower-cluster; either he stands at the head of all,‡ or he fades in the forest."

"The diamond, though senseless, bursts into flame at the touch of the sun's rays; then how can the man of fiery spirit endure wrong from another?"

"The water-drop lying on heated iron is known no more, even as to its name; the same, when it lies on the leaf in the lotus-bed, shines in the semblance of a pearl; when it falls into an oyster-shell in the ocean under Arcturus, it becomes

* See above, p. 108.

† A fabulous mountain, supposed to form the centre of the world.

‡ The comparison is with the garland of flowers worn on the head.

a real pearl.* The characters of base, commonplace, and noble men are as a rule made by their associations."

"As he joyfully munches a foul-smelling, loathsome human bone swarming with worms and wet with spittle, as though it were of exquisite savour, the dog will feel no scruple, even though he see the king of the gods himself standing at his side. A base creature recks not of the worthlessness of his possessions."

"Perchance one may get oil in the sands by stoutly pressing them; and perchance the thirsty may find a drink of water in the mirage; haply a traveller may discover even a horn on a hare; but nothing can win over the mind of the confirmed fool."

"Charity done in secret, eager courtesy to the visitor of his house, silence after doing kindness and public mention after receiving it, modesty in fortune, conversation without spice of insolence, —who taught good men this rule of life, hard as a sword's edge to tread?"

"The moon darkened by day, the mistress whose youth has fled, the pool that has lost its lilies, the speechless mouth in a comely form, the prince caring only for wealth, the good man ever in distress, the base in the King's court—these are seven stabs in my heart."

* A common Eastern belief. The constellation Arcturus (*Svāti*) comes on the ecliptic about October 22.

"Strange it is that he has the same perfect senses, the same name, the same unweakened mind, the same speech—and yet this same man, deprived of the warmth of wealth, becomes in an instant another!"

"Let high birth go to the nether world, and all merits sink even lower, virtue be cast down from a precipice, pedigree be consumed by fire, the thunderbolt descend swiftly upon insolent valour—only let us have riches! For if that one thing be lacking, all these merits are no better than a bit of grass."

As we have seen, Bhartṛi-hari sometimes finds in his doctrine of predestination an encouragement to the manly spirit. At other times, however, it suggests gloomier thoughts. "Is it the fault of the spring that no foliage stands on the *karīra*-bush? * Is the sun to be blamed if the owl has no vision in daylight? Is the cloud to be chided because its water-drops fall not down the throat of the *chātaka*? † Who can wipe out what Fate has once written on the brow?" But even Fate is nothing more than a blind instrument for the power of Karma, the Works which fetter the soul to the world. So he exclaims: "Shall we do homage to the gods? But surely they too are

* A leafless shrub, *Capparis aphylla,* Roxburgh.

† A bird which, according to tradition, seeks its drink only from the falling raindrops; and of these it can swallow but very few.

vassals of stern Fate. Should Fate be worshipped? But it again is the mere allotter of the ordained issues of our Works. What need is there of gods and Fate, if the issues depend on our Works? Homage then to Works, over which even Fate has no power!" And in grim satire he writes: "Homage to Work, which has confined Brahmā like a potter inside the pot of the world, cast Vishṇu into the inextricable maze of his ten incarnations, made Śiva beg for alms with a skull in his hand, and sends the Sun everlastingly roaming through the sky!"

But as the Shakspere of the dramas was also the Shakspere of the sonnets, so also this sage man of the world has left in his "Century of Love" a record of passion which in its changeful moods of lyric fervour recalls Heine's "Buch der Lieder." Again and again, when he had drained the cup of passion to the dregs, he sought peace for his soul in religion; but his heart was still restless under the ragged gown of the monk, and time after time drove him back to the world that he had hoped to abandon.

The spirit of the hermitage is expressed by him in his *Vairāgya-śataka*, the "Century of the Stilled Soul." In this he touches the themes usual to singers of *vanitas vanitatum*, but with unusual earnestness and dignity, telling "the old, old story that is ever new":

"Day by day with the coming and going of the sun life fades away; in labour heavy with the burdens of manifold tasks time is sped unmarked; dread arises not at sight of birth, age, mishap, and death—the world has drunk the maddening wine of heedlessness, and is distraught!"

"They from whom we were born have long since gone; they with whom we grew up have likewise been sent down the path of memory; and now we are in our estate like to trees upon the sandy bank of a stream, each day more ready to fall."

"Ended is the yearning for delights, forspent is pride of manhood; friends and peers that were dear as life are now gone heavenward; slowly one rises by the staff, and eyes are barred with thick darkness—and withal, alas! the outworn body dreads Death's coming!"

"A little while a child—then a little while a youthful gallant—a little while in need of substance—then a little while in wealthy estate—then with age-worn limbs at the end of his life's wanderings Man, like a stage-player, his body garbed in wrinkles, passes away behind the curtain of Hades." *

"Alas, brother, the mighty king, the train of barons, the witty court at his side, the maidens with faces like the moon's orb, the haughty troop

* Thus Shakspere's "Seven Ages of Man" was anticipated in the seventh century.

of princes, the minstrels, the tales,—homage to Time, by whose will all this has passed into mere memory ! "

Once he turns for a moment to the old love with a sad epigram : " Erstwhile we twain deemed that thou wast I and I was thou ; how comes it now that thou art thou and I am I ? "

But these reminders of the past are seldom heard. His thoughts are for the most part turned to a blessed future, and at times he writes in measures of stately harmony recalling something of the spirit both of Wordsworth and of Francis of Assisi, yet remaining ever Indian :

" When shall we sit peacefully in the voiceless nights upon the divine river's sandy shore white-paved with moonbeams in glittering swell, and in loathing of the expanse of life lift up our voice in the cry of ' Śiva, Śiva ! ' with eyes flooded by many a joy-born tear ? "

" What profit scriptures, law-books, reading of pious stories, bulky tomes of lore, and the medley of works and rites that win for reward lodging in a hut of a village in Paradise ? Save the entrance into the abode of bliss in the soul, which is like Time's fire sweeping away the works that burden life with sorrow, all is but trafficker's craft."

" O mother Earth, father Wind, friend Sunshine, kinsman Water, brother Sky, for the last time I clasp my hands in reverence before you. The might of all error is overthrown in me by the stainless radiant knowledge from the rich store of good works born of your comradeship, and I sink into the Supernal Spirit."

Published by

Facsimile Publisher
Ashok Vihar, Delhi-110052 (India)
Website: www.facsimilepublisher.com

Distributed by

Gyan Books Pvt. Ltd.
5, Ansari Road, Daryaganj, New Delhi-110002 (India)
E-mail: books@gyanbooks.com, Website: www.gyanbooks.com